ELEVATE

ELEVATE

ELEVATE YOUR THINKING
ELEVATE YOUR LIFE

TAMIEN DYSART

Elevate
Copyright ©2023 Tamien Dysart
Published by Think 3D Solutions

All rights reserved. No portion of this book may be reproduced, stored in a retrieval system, or transmitted in any form or by any means—electronic, mechanical, photocopy, recording, scanning, or other—except for brief quotations in critical reviews or articles, without the prior written permission of the author or publisher.

ISBN: 979-8-9873130-0-8 (paperback)
ISBN: 979-8-9873130-1-5 (hardcover)
ISBN: 979-8-9873130-2-2 (e-book)

Cover artwork designed using assets from Freepik.com
Chapter artwork designed by pikisuperstar / Freepik

Edited by Daniel Card
Book Design by James Woosley, FreeAgentPress.com

CONTENTS

ELEVATE

Thinking (think-ing)
verb

The process of using one's mind to consider
or reason about something.

I have a recurring nightmare where I'm at the end of my life and
sitting around in a retirement community or on my porch in my
rocking chair and replaying all my regrets and missed opportunities.

Nothing scares me more than the thought of being left at the end
of my life and facing the pain of regret, knowing I had so much
more to offer, or to achieve.

So, I spend a lot of my time thinking about what it would feel like
to sit on a front porch in my golden years and feel confident that I
made the most of this opportunity called life.

Have you ever thought about what your front-porch rocking chair moment would feel like?

What would you be proud of?

What would you regret?

What would you do differently now, knowing that moment is on its way?

What would it take to look back on a life "well-lived?"

I believe that a life of regret is one that is filled with an abundance of unintentional living.

"A life of regret is one that is filled with unintentional living."

If you are honest with yourself, when no-one is around – just you and your inner most thoughts, how intentionally are you living?

Jim Rohn, the famous entrepreneur and motivational speaker, talked about two things that drive human beings – pleasure or pain.

In my experience, most people spend most of their time trying to avoid pain, because pain is uncomfortable.

However, it's impossible to completely avoid pain altogether by pursuing pleasure or comfort. The reality is we face pain no matter what, and in one of two ways. We can embrace the pain of discipline, or we can carry the pain of regret.

> *"We must all suffer from one of two pains: the pain of discipline or the pain of regret. The difference is discipline weighs ounces while regret weighs tons."*
>
> JIM ROHN

If this sounds harsh or unrealistic, I want you to put this book down and go visit a retirement home. Go talk to as many people as you can and listen to them describe their life and the choices they made. You will get a newfound perspective on the word, "regret."

Now I want you to ask yourself a question, "are you preparing for and pursuing an intentional and successful life?"

In my experience, there are many people who haven't given this question the depth of consideration it deserves. It's not a daydream or wishing about what you want in the future, it is preparation and an examination of your expectations, commitment, and actions.

At the foundation of all of that, and what you need to take away from this book is – your thoughts. Examine your thoughts, your intentions, beliefs, and actions – but it starts with your thoughts.

I want you to consider your thoughts the same way a farmer would approach growing and harvesting crops. Just "having" or being exposed to good thoughts is a start, but it's not enough.

A farmer doesn't just throw seeds on the ground and wait for a harvest to appear. There is an intentional process. They go through a process, they prepare the soil, they tend to its growth, and they maintain, water, and nourish the growth of their seeds and soil.

To start preparing soil a farmer must remove the rocks and till the land. Then there is preparation and planning into where the seeds are planted so they grow. Then, the consistent work to ensure the seeds are properly watered, fertilized, and free of weeds to nourish the growth. Finally, after months of work, patience and process, the harvest is ready.

In the same way, being able to sow, grow and harvest seeds of wisdom takes work, patience, and process.

If you look back over the last few years of your life, what seeds of wisdom have you encountered or collected?

What have you done with them? Are you planting, nourishing, and growing these seeds?

TEMPERATURE CHECK

I want to challenge you to do something with me right now.

Say out loud to yourself,

"I am okay being average!"

How did that feel? If you went out of your way to pick up this book and get this far, I'm fairly certain you are a high achiever, and that sentence doesn't feel great.

The reality is, even though that sentence makes many of us uncomfortable, by definition, most people are average. Many people haven't understood the time, commitment, or path by which they will achieve more of their potential.

My hope is that as you read this book, you will begin to believe that you are worthy, and worth it, and should commit to unlocking your higher potential.

I hope that you can pause and examine where you are, without judgment. Are you not where you want to be in life? Have you had a hard year? Perhaps you are winning left and right, but know you could be doing more?

Regardless of your assessment of where you are, you can do something that moves the needle forward.

I want you to know that you can, and should put in the work, to be your best self. You owe it to yourself, if no one else, to be the best version of you possible.

Over the rest of this book, you will be challenged to examine your thinking, your intention, your process, and the results. You can and should expect to spend intentional time reflecting on what you read even before you begin to work through the Power Thoughts in the second part of this book.

Let's begin.

EVERYONE HAS THOUGHTS — FEW PEOPLE THINK

Thinking is a verb, it's an active process. Thoughts, however, happen regardless of intention. Thoughts are a passive and automatic occurrence. Everyone has thoughts – not nearly as many people spend intentional time *thinking*.

In the same way that you don't have to *make* your heartbeat, or your blood to flow through your body, you don't *have to*, do anything for thoughts to fill your mind.

Not convinced? Try it. Right now, take 30 seconds and stop thinking…

…how did that go?

I imagine it didn't.

The reason is, our brains continue to produce thoughts, with or without our intention.

Studies done by Dr. Fred Luskin at Stanford University found that the average individual has around 60,000 thoughts a day. Yes, 60,000. Let that sink in for a moment.

Dr. Luskin also suggested that over 90% of these thoughts are repetitive, or a "rinse and repeat" from the day before.

This is a primary reason why you might hear that "people don't change." It is so difficult to escape the past version of yourself because your thought patterns happen in a memorized sequence, thus forming strong thought pathways that are woven into your identity.

When we really unpack the world in which we came from, all of who you were – how you thought, and your belief systems had next to nothing to do with you up until the age of 18.

We didn't choose the family we were born into. We didn't choose most of the experiences we had or the schools we went to. Even though most of us believe that we chose our friends, it was still from a selection of people who were in the same neighborhood or school. Most of them coming from similar economic backgrounds, similar families who had similar interests or beliefs.

This is why one of the biggest barriers to stepping into the next best version of yourself is intentional thinking. The core of that is people mistaking *thoughts, for thinking.*

> **"Don't mistake your thoughts, for your thinking."**
>
> THINK 3D

Thinking is a like a muscle, it needs to be exercised and developed. If we're being completely honest, most people we engage with all around us are just going through the motions. Yes, they use their brain in the work they do, the conversations they have, and their day-to-day activities, but realistically most spend little or no time with a focused intent on elevating their thinking.

This is no different than the need to work out to get in shape or training a muscle. It takes time, commitment, and intentionality to develop this part of our brain. Without it, we're left to fall back on the passive thoughts we have (to the tune of 60,000 a day), that were informed by our environment, our background and the people around us. No wonder so many people spend time wishing for or wondering why they don't have the successful life they want.

FINDING THE TIME TO COMMIT

We're going to start this by being super honest – you have time. All of us have time.

We live in a day and age where we love saying how "busy" we are, when the truthful question should lead us to, busy doing what? If we want some honest insight on what, we don't have to look any further than our phones to see how much time we spend on fruitless engagement, the number of videos watched or what we're doing in the first and last hours of our days.

In any given week, you have 168 hours. Most of us can and do justify that we're too busy or that we can't carve out a few hours of intentional development to improve our overall life. At this point in our life, are we willing to truly come face to face with the question – is it worth it for me to make the commitment to the life I say I desire to have?

If your answer was yes, then where and when will you find and dedicate the time to commit to exercising your mind? To reflect and plant these seeds into your mental soil? If saying *"I'm okay being average"* didn't sit well with you (which it probably didn't if you're still reading up to this point), then you can and will be able to find time to carve out and dedicate to being exceptional.

You have the time. It is a matter of priority. Be honest with yourself, you know that things that hold the highest priority you simply make time for. Like those moments where you felt you couldn't carve out time for yourself, then a loved one passes away, and you're forced to be away from your "busyness." Or when a child or spouse has an emergency or left their wallet at the store, and you step away and make time. Life somehow managed to move forward, you managed to get through that project or those emails – even though you made time for something else.

So, how do you spend your 168 hours each week? In the Netflix documentary *The Social Dilemma*, it's suggested that the average person is spending approximately 3.5 hours a day on their phone. Add the amount of time watching television or on our other devices surfing the internet, and it's quickly clear, we all have time.

Now, how much time you have varies, some of us, even you might be terribly busy. However, if getting to where we "say" we want to go or be in life is truly a priority, we'll prioritize and dedicate the time to engage in activities that will carry us to our destination or accomplishments.

Okay, so we got through some honest insight and are aware that there's a gap in the way we use our time.

Now what?

One of my favorite quotes is from Les Brown, one of the world's most renowned motivational speakers. He said that "Want shows up in conversation. Expectations shows up in behavior."

> **"Want shows up in conversation. Expectations show up in behavior."**
>
> **LES BROWN**

It is easy to sit around and talk about what we want. This takes no effort, and it is fun to dream about what we wish we had in life. However, if the steps needed to build those dreams and aspirations aren't showing up in our daily behaviors, we are allowing our dreams to remain nothing more than wishful thinking.

One way you can do this, is to start using your phone differently. You must start using things like your phone (which you're probably on more than you need to be), differently. Think about how you could use your phone to set a reminder to spend 15 minutes preparing for the next day, and another 15 to reflect on the day you had. Or you could use your phone to disable notifications, set timers for apps, and being able to take small, simple steps towards elevating your thinking, and creating time for it.

This leads us to a key of developing power thoughts. By elevating our thinking within the context of simple things we're already doing, and doing them repeatedly, we begin to build a process and a new way of thinking that will elevate our lives.

Ask yourself – is the future you want to create worth an hour and a half a week?

Go back and read "I'm okay with being average again…," then answer that question.

It's commitment time.

Right now, reach out to 3 people you trust and tell them that you want to grow, and you want to achieve more. Share that you've been reading this book and that one of the things you need to do is spend 20 minutes reflecting, *thinking,* and investing into yourself each week. Tell them that you are done with excuses instead of results in your life and you are asking for their help. All you need is a straightforward text or call each week to hold you accountable to your 20 minutes. Because without the commitment to growth each week, you aren't going to achieve what you know you are capable of and want.

Let me quick jump in and speak to the majority who won't do this. I too know this feeling well. I have been that person who, at a sub-conscious level, didn't want to be held accountable. I did not follow through on so many of the things that books challenged me to do. I have been intentional about minimizing the action step I ask of readers because I know that most of them won't follow-through.

Up until this point, there has been no action steps and there will be very few outside of engaging in the weekly process of Power Thoughts.

My point is that it doesn't get any easier than this.

I'll make the ask even simpler, even if you have 1 person. You need to have a conversation and ask someone to check in every week, just a text or a reminder, to make sure you are staying committed to yourself and your goals.

If you can't do *that*, I am not sure how effective the rest of this book is going to be for you. This should be a point of reflection and exploration as you challenge yourself and ask, "why not?," when you think about the commitment and work to reach a higher level of potential.

There is no magic bullet to becoming better. It takes doing the work.

For the better part of 15 years of personal development, I hoarded more and more knowledge, but I did only a fraction of the work to apply this knowledge.

So again, if you are choosing to skip past this basic accountability exercise, learn to be okay being average (again – there is nothing wrong with being average unless you're not okay being average) because your brains laziness is fighting for you to stay the same and if we won't do the work, nothing works.

I have studied out success extensively and accountability is one of the most common characteristics of almost every person you would consider "successful."

If for whatever reason you still are skeptical, I would challenge you to put this book down and go study it out for yourself. Unpack the lives of people you admire the most and I am positive you will discover critical moments where those individuals CHOSE to develop the resolve to push through, despite their something or someone trying to hold them back. Once they had those break-throughs, they were never the same.

I am confident that you can follow in those footsteps to become that next better version of who you can become. Let's continue the journey...

2

JUMPING THE HURDLES

What's stopping you?

Something I have come to believe wholeheartedly the more people I meet is that we all have higher potential inside of us, and that we are all capable of remarkable things. So why do so many people settle for less than their fullest potential?

It's important to note that when we're talking about "what's stopping us," or why we haven't taken steps towards our fullest potential that we do so safely, and without judgment. This isn't about rating a performance or beating yourself or others up for excuses – this is simply a "you are here" marker. Because without knowing where we are, we cannot know where we are going.

Far too often I see people avoiding honest assessments due to either a lack of confidence or a lack of reality. They either overplay where they are at because they know the lingo, they share the inspirational posts, they are "hustling" or "grinding" all the time – you know the type; or they beat themselves up with poor self-talk and negativity because they are hypercritical of themselves.

Something that drives this often-inaccurate perspective is our feelings; something which subconsciously dictates a substantial part of our lives.

Think about if someone were to ask you, "Is today better than it was 3 months ago?," the majority would start off responding with, "I feel like…"

The hard part of this is that feelings are subjective, and often fleeting. Meaning, your entire perspective of something might be completely tainted by how you *feel* in the moment.

Regardless of how well something went, or how much you did, if you *feel* it didn't go well, or you were clouded by negative emotion, your perspective of it may be completely inaccurate.

By starting from a foundation based in honest, judgment free assessment of our progress and achievements, we move from basing our perspective in our *feeling* and begin to base them in the clear reality of where we are at. Which allows us to move forward and make adjustments more effectively.

Another hurdle that holds many people back from more of their potential is their belief system. Earlier we shared that most of our belief systems, including our identity, thought patterns, and decision making was developed without much of our individual intention or awareness.

A belief, at its core, is simply a sustained way of thinking. Over time, we come to accept this as fact deep into our conscious and subconscious. If you look at religious views, political opinions, or what we view as "success" – you can see that most of what we believe to be true about the world has come from a sustained, or repeated pattern of thought.

You more than likely formed a pattern of thinking based on what you were exposed to long before you even consciously began to question or understand any of it. Depending on where you grew up, your home life, your friends, and your family's beliefs, you were immersed in groups that shared similar or overlapping beliefs.

If you grew up in a family that was mostly Republican or Democratic, Christian or Muslim, had racial biases, these beliefs were the basis of your earliest thoughts and experiences.

The byproduct of which, was your earliest, and even your current belief system that you have carried into adulthood. If someone asks you *why* you believe the things you do, you will likely have a response ready about how it aligns with your values or an experience that shaped your thought. However, when you look deeper, the seeds were planted by our environment and exposure.

Now of course, along the way your beliefs have evolved to some degree. Take a moment to look back and find moments where your beliefs changed, even just slightly.

More than likely, your beliefs changed when your environment, or exposure did as well. It could have been a new friend group, a move to a new area or part of the country, or a life-changing experience. The common thread here, is that *something* or *someone* had an impact on you and changed your way of thinking, it didn't just happen by itself.

I'm trying to get at two things. First, the understanding that for most of us, our current way of thinking, our actions, and our perspective is derived from our belief system. Your life, the outcomes of your thoughts, actions, and perspective, in a way reflects your beliefs. Second, the belief system we base most of our decisions on, for most of our life is absorbed from the environments and people around us.

These two realizations lead us to the question – how does a person change the trajectory or path of their life? By introducing new thoughts and changing the way they think.

Take a minute to pause and think about what new thoughts or ways of thinking you have intentionally introduced into your life over the last 3-6 months?

If you have several, that's amazing, and well done. If you can't find an example, or aren't sure, that's okay too. Regardless of the past, what is happening in our current reality, or what we have coming – you have the power to *choose* your focus and start placing attention on how and what you want to think about.

This is challenging though. Shifting a mindset, building a new way of thinking, or returning to a healthier way of thinking takes energy and intention. It goes outside of how our brains are wired to function. For the earliest parts of human history, our brains kept us from the unknown as a means of survival. Even throughout modern history, it is only through the courage of curiosity of those who defied the fear and went first.

Comfort, mediocrity, fear – all keep us in a lethargic state of "good enough." To break free from this requires deliberately challenging and elevating your mindset and your paradigm. A paradigm is simply your pattern or way of thinking and making decisions. They sit at the foundation of our belief system and dictate how we see and navigate the world. However, they are nothing more than the result of a sustained thought and way of thinking.

You begin to shift a paradigm when you focus intentional and sustained thinking on something new, or something you desire. This anchors new thoughts towards a specific destination and allows you to start making decisions and forming actions that support and validate this way of thinking.

In this context, I want you to consider pointing your thoughts, and shifting your paradigms to support the version of you that you want to see emerge over the next few months and year.

As you focus intentionally on the future, and the person you want to be, the life you want to have – you will elevate your way of thinking and begin to see a path to your future. Which allows you to make decisions differently, you can see that obstacles are steppingstones towards elevating your life.

3

BE OBSERVANT

Let's dive into the importance of being observant for a moment.

When was the last time you closely saw the causes and effects of what's happening in your life, and the lives of the people closest to you or those you see most often?

What I mean by that is have you truly examined, or observed the way you and others are living and making decisions?

You might be highly observant, that's a quality trait, however, take this moment to reflect on the world you live in. Of the hundreds, or perhaps thousands of people you know, how many would you say are truly "living their best life?"

We ask people this question a lot, and it is rare to get more than a few people to raise their hand in acknowledging they know at least 5 people in their spheres of relationships and acquaintances who are genuinely living their best life.

What I think this points to is the fact that at a large scale, people live in conformity to the masses. Which means we settle for someone else's definition of success, or we settle to a level that's comfortable for the people around us, often without intentionally realizing we are doing so.

Without seeing this impact around us, we will never realize that we aren't making the necessary decisions to create and design our life *on purpose*. Simply put, a lack of investment towards the future you want leads to a lack luster life.

I truly don't believe that anyone sets out with the intentional mindset of being mediocre, or "good enough." The results of a life that falls short of their potential isn't something they meant to happen. It is simply collateral damage, or unintended consequences, but it's a cycle and you can trace this cycle back over generations.

I look at my mother's life and see that her parents were tremendously affected by growing up in the great depression. This affected their aspirations and mentality to simply being grateful for what you have. From this, my mom carried with her a "just be happy to have a decent paying job" view of work. Sure, there is power in gratitude and perspective, but this belief that shaped the way she made decisions was based out of the fear and insecurity her parents carried from their experiences in times of significant uncertainty and challenge. She was a hard-working woman who always went to work, always without complaint, yet didn't expect much out of life beyond what working to pay the bills gave her.

This observation isn't meant to make us feel bad, it's simply to acknowledge things as they are. Again, it is observing the cause and effect of the things in our life, rather than taking them at face value. If we can learn to aspire for more because the observation of others who simply settled for bare minimum or for safety, we can elevate our lives.

To put a different perspective on this I'm going to ask you a question: Do you think your children, or your future children would want to live the life you lead today?

We ask this question to people when we are training them, and the overwhelming majority says no. So, if we don't think our kids or future kids would want the life we live currently, what are we passing along to this next generation?

I remember when my oldest daughter was going into high school, I told her to be observant of the people around her, because they will make most of the mistakes for her to learn from.

Of course, she, as do all of us, still had to learn a few lessons the hard way, but she exercised a great deal of observation and now she's far surpassed many of the same people she grew up around because of her decisions. Part of this is informed by her observations, and the thoughts, thinking and beliefs she was exposed to growing up in a home where I was consistently challenging her to be her best self.

Again, I believe that a life of regret is one that is filled with an abundance of unintentional living. I remember visiting my grandfather when he was in a small-town nursing home. The smell, the gloom, the heaviness of people in the final years of their life was painfully clear. I saw hallways with people getting wheeled out into the doorway of their room and the expressionless emotion upon their faces. I couldn't help but wonder how heavy the regrets of their life was; and now they find themselves in a place of being able to do next to nothing about it.

That experience was one that gave me a baseline to look at how I thought about legacy and the life I want to live while I still have the ability to almost fully impact the outcome. Currently in my early forties, I am trying to ask and answer intentional questions. I often reflect to what it will feel like sitting in a rocking chair at age 80. What type of life would I have to have lived, that would leave me with a smile of satisfaction that it was indeed a great life? What type of regrets might I have wished I had done differently?

With these few, but simple questions, I have a baseline of building the kind of life that not only will I be proud of but will also provide a foundation for others within my sphere to realize that they too can and should be designing their life with intention. This is removing the possibility of regret while we still have sand in the top half of life's hourglass.

Before moving on, I would challenge you to pause and *observe* your life in the same way. What type of opportunities come to mind? If you stay on your current trajectory, will you be left with regret later in life? One can look back 6-12 months and estimate their trajectory to this point, and then look forward over the next 6-12 months to get an approximation of where you'll be. Does that vision and version of your life concern you at all? If you see any room for improvement at all, keep reading. Let's elevate.

4

WHAT IS ON THE "OTHER SIDE"

When you pause and think about the possibilities for your life, what gets you excited? I'm not talking about spaces of simply wishing, but things you believe are possible that would truly add real value to the quality of and joy in your life.

It's been said that we overestimate what we can get done in a year, yet grossly underestimate what we can do in 5 years. Looking back 5 years from today, I am sure you can see how and where you have clearly grown as well as some areas you feel that are about the same.

We all tend to lose something after childhood, the eager anticipation of growing a year older. It goes well beyond just the excitement of cake and presents, but the added benefits and privileges' of being older. Kids are excited to hit milestones like hitting double digits, becoming a teenager, being old enough to drive or get a job, turning 18 and becoming an adult, and turning 21 so that all of life's freedoms are available to them. However, once most adults get past 21, there is rarely celebrations outside of our decade milestones. There's no anticipation of growth, opportunity, and we begin just trudging through life, hoping for just better than okay, or "not bad."

Take the simple premise and promise of this book – to elevate your thinking and elevate your life.

What type of person would you become if you did nothing more but took one powerful quote, or challenge, truly soaked it in and intentionally began to evaluate and *think* on it and how it could have relevance in your life and implemented just one thing? Then repeated this each week for all 52 weeks in the year.

American poet and humorist Oliver Wendell Holmes noted that,

> ### *"Man's mind, stretched to a new idea, never goes back to its original dimension."*

What version of you is waiting on the other side of 52 weeks of intention? It's hard to spend that kind of time and investment exploring and rewiring your thinking and still remain the same version of yourself.

Imagine for a moment you are walking through the supermarket with your 10-year-old child, when they ask if they can have some cookies. You patiently and kindly tell them no. They go ahead and throw themselves on the ground throwing a tantrum like a toddler. This isn't behavior you would expect from a 10-year-old, and you're more than likely expressing that to them, in perhaps a less than patient manner now.

The reason we can expect that a 10-year-old child doesn't throw themselves on the ground in the supermarket when told they cannot have a cookie and that they act their age is they have had a few more years of growth and development from when they were 3 years old, and tantrums were more common. They should "know better" because you've held this expectation that they understand getting older means getting more communicative, growing, becoming more mature and overall improving.

When did we stop having these expectations of becoming a better version of ourselves? Countless studies share that the average person does truly little self-development once their years of formal education are completed. Why? Without a plan or expectation of ourselves to continue to grow and improve what happens? Look around and you'll see countless examples of people who have abandoned a dream, or chosen not to take a risk, or who haven't grown past limiting beliefs.

When I look back on the history of the United States, I am amazed at the massive ambition, relentless curiosity, and sheer willpower of the men and women who shaped our country into the global juggernaut we see today.

It was with similar dreams, ambition and willpower that many of our ancestors pushed through hardship and uncertainty with nothing more than a desire for better.

Fast forward to today and we can see clearly that we have a serious cause of not dreaming, even though we live in a country that was built on dreams.

Of course, you still have your titans of entrepreneurial spirit such as Elon Musk, Jeff Bezos, Mark Zuckerberg, and others. However, the vast majority have left the ambition and pure desire for better to those select few whom we like to assign to be "special" or having a level of intelligence that is beyond our grasp.

Now I'm not saying that we all can or should aspire to that type or level of influence or success. There clearly are differences between these multi-billionaires and people who land in the middle class.

These differences go far beyond financial prosperity, and into holistic properties some of which involves genuinely loving your life. If we don't give our attention to what we want and therefore set a level of intention, then we're leaving the outcomes and possibilities of our lives up to chance.

I would imagine that many people haven't given any considerable amount of thought to what they, and their life would look like with even just small investments like 20 minutes of intentional reflection each week.

I could probably sum up most of this book by saying that it's the incremental introduction of habits, positivity, reflection, and intentional thinking that leads to taking action, which leads us to the life we desire and our **Higher Potential**.

How can we start to spend intentional time, focused in on what we believe is possible to achieve and look at what one year of elevated thinking and living looks like?

We start by getting specific with what we want to achieve.

Challenge yourself to spend time building a vision of what the "next best version" looks like. How would your life be better than it is now? Who's impacted for the better by that version of you?

Step 1 – get to know what you want to see on the other side.

Step 2 – get realistic with what it will take to get there.

Step 3 – get committed and start.

THE POWER OF "WHITE SPACE"

We don't have to look any further than trying to spend 20 minutes alone in our minds to realize just how much distractions have grown to be a major obstacle working against us in developing the lives we want.

Companies are dialing in at an accelerated pace learning how to get us more and more addicted to the latest app on our phones or getting us to spend hours mindlessly watching shows.

With this trend only getting worse, we must question and seek out ways that we can cut the umbilical cord from technology when we want to.

Paraphrasing a statement from the Netflix documentary *The Social Dilemma*, "our brain is the greatest supercomputer ever created;

however, on the other side of those screens are warehouses of super-computers" – thus our brains stand no chance! (At least not without clear and present intentionality)

The real secret of success in life is found through self-discovery.

If we aren't taking the time to get to know who we really are, what we truly desire, and why we want these things, we will continue living life on rinse and repeat from the preconditioning we came with.

We can see just how big of a problem we have in society when at almost any given free moment, most people do what? Reach for their phones.

Got a 30-minute wait at a restaurant? Waiting rooms filled with people glued to their devices. Stopped a red light? Let me quick check my feed to see how many likes I got. The list could go on and on.

If we truly want to live our best life possible, based solely on how *we personally* define what it means to live our best life, we must allow time and space to resonate with our higher truth and how it "could" apply to and improve our lives.

It isn't hard to wrap our heads around the idea that if we continue to do what we've always done, or even what others have always done, we will continue to get what we (or they) have always gotten.

Again, unless we're wanting to rinse and repeat the past we've come from or follow in the footsteps of those we've been influenced by, then carving out the time and the space to go within ourselves isn't a choice, it is an absolute must.

Being from the Midwest, it isn't hard to see how we've arrived at this place of complacency or settling.

Living in South Dakota, we often complain about cold and long winters. I often joke that though we complain, we suck it up better than anyone.

Looking back at the cloth from which we're cut here in the upper Midwest, we come from a long line of people built for 'long suffering'. As we complain when temperatures get below zero or we get inches of snow, imagine what it was like living here 100 years ago.

One had better be equipped with the ability of long suffering, or they simply wouldn't make it. This mentality, in many ways unfortunately, has caused the masses to settle for "good enough" simply because it is "better than." This simply cannot remain as any level of standard that we still are okay with.

Based on the fact that every single human walking this planet is a unique individual, we too then should be seeking out how to live as such.

Life should be a customized journey that is designed with elevated levels of enjoyment on as frequent of a basis as possible. No one else has walked the exact same path as you or had all the same experiences you have had.

Along those lines, no other person can show us exactly how we should live this life we are currently living. Of course, we can and should examine the lives of others and draw inspiration from things they may have carried out as we craft our version of living a life well lived, but it still must have a high level of determining what is right for us!

What does it take to do this?

White space.

White space that exists in between the everyday busyness of living.

I'm not talking about leaving everything behind to visit a Tibetan monastery for a month or trying to find hours of time to spend in nature. Though these types of things do have tremendous value, it is not practical for most people.

And if people aren't given real, tangible, practical solutions to step toward creating a better life for themselves, it again becomes far too easy to fall into the trap of "good enough."

If we really unpack what is happening to most of society, the majority are finding themselves unhappy because they've adapted to being mimicked versions of other people, never discovering their own truth.

It is often said, and often true, that we are and reflect the sum of the 5 closest people we hang around. Looking back over our lives, at various stages who were the individuals that made up the 5 closest people you hung around?

For most of our childhood it was our parents. From here, as we enter our teenage years, our friend groups become our life. In this stage, most of our friends are going to come from similar circumstances and thus common ways of thinking. By the time we are well into being adults and have full control and say so on who are friends are and where we spend our time, we aren't far from simply mirroring the environments that we had come from.

Of course, there are exceptions to the rule, but the majority follow the rule. Having a heightened awareness of this helps us to find the clear and present need to not just create space, but to make it a priority, and dedicate time to do it.

The most successful people in the world have the same 24 hours a day that all of us do, however they simply value their time differently and make sure to carve out time and space to go within. Time to step into the next greater version of themselves and the lives that they want through choosing thoughts, actions, and beliefs that elevate them.

One of the best ways to finding this precious white space is through meditation. Though I would consider myself a novice and only first discovered its power and potential just a short few years ago, I have learned that true self-discovery is next to impossible without this practice. Regardless of your familiarity with the power of meditation, I highly encourage you to look at both the science behind it as well as the endless examples of successful people referencing this being among their common daily practices.

Like anything new, it isn't the easiest thing at first. It takes practice, and persistence in order to get good at it.

Thinking back to the challenge earlier in the book to try and stop your thoughts, you realize that it is nearly impossible.

However, meditation can help us learn and develop the ability to slow our habitual thinking down and refocus in the moment to create new patterns of intentional thinking.

I'll leave this conversation on mediation short because there is a plethora of apps, books, and information that can help you discover what works best for you. However, I'll say it again for clarity, if you don't learn to meditate or quiet your mind, you simply will not be able to step into your **Higher Potential** because you will be limited by your old patterns of thinking.

As we have discussed already, our lives have been shaped, molded and formed without much intentionality.

If we are to step into our "best life" by design, we will need to adopt the wisdom spoken of in the Bible, Romans 12:2 advising us to "…be not conformed to the patterns of this world: but be ye transformed by the renewing of your mind."

We've covered beliefs, thoughts and thinking, hurdles, and the need for intention. We know that without intentionally elevating our thinking, and our life we will fall back on someone else's definition of success, or what the world tells us we need to be doing, saying, or feeling.

In order to break free from this – you need to create a space where you can think, process, and examine uninterrupted.

Obviously, renewing our minds is one of the core tenets of this book, taking seeds of wisdom and creating space for it to soak in and be fertilized in the mental soil of our minds. This process is accelerated by your ability to step into and engage this white space.

THE POWER OF JOURNALING

Look back one year from today. How have you grown? What's different, or what have you done differently that points to this growth?

For most of our adult lives, development or growth is measured in 5- or 10-year increments. Your "twenties," "thirties," "forties" and so on; or your mid-thirties, mid-forties, etc.

When you stop and think about it, that is a lot of time. Even breaking down one year which consists of 365 days, 52 weeks, 8,760 hours – there is a ton of time, growth, and change that happens.

However, in the absence of any evidence (outside of pictures if we've made some noticeable physical changes), it can be easy to see how these massive blocks of time are simply lumped together. Especially when we aren't *using* that time intentionally.

Taking this another step, how would you articulate that you have improved the way you *think* over the last year?

This hits home for me. In my mid-twenties I developed an appreciation for the power of reading books but had no real, intentional application of the things I was learning. There are significant blocks of time that I wasn't able to articulate any difference in myself one year from the next.

> ### *Journaling gives us unmistakable evidence of our growth and a log of what is happening daily in our lives.*

I would remind you that goal setting and time management still play a huge role in *seeing* and *tracking* your growth. Being able to journal, however, gives us an opportunity to track daily, the way we *think* and how we are growing.

One of the greatest tools that high-level athletes have at their disposal is the ability to watch themselves for hours and hours on film. Watching game film shows them areas they can improve on and adjust, even details as small as moving a foot or adjusting a posture slightly.

When you journal with consistency and intention, it becomes your game film. You get critical details about how you can continue to grow. The better your journaling, the better your game film and the better your performance.

Journaling also helps you keep track of your record. Many people struggle to muster the drive to pursue their goals because they seem so difficult, or far away. Yet, looking back over our lives, how many things have we overcome in the past, but have now forgotten about on the other side? This is why you need to see your winning record.

You will be reminded that you indeed can conquer the challenge in front of you. The past can be fuel for your confidence. We often tend to forget and overlook how far we come and the things we have conquered.

Leveraging this mindset, helps keep us growing; knowing the results will work out, not always in the moment, but in the end. Instead of focusing on the distance between us and our desires, we can simply focus on the mindset that we've had in the past when facing similar challenges.

The degree to which we journal or how often is up to everyone to decide for themselves. However, the point is about tracking our progress. It gives us clearer points of reference as we navigate our way through our months and years.

My journey of journaling has gone through several iterations. I tried long-form journaling and struggled with it. I'm not a natural writer… if you're reading this you can tell. After trying to mimic what other people created left me stuck, more often than not, I had to customize what worked best for me.

The pressure of "doing it right" fell away once I got to the core of what I needed to get out of it, and just started to *do it*. There is no right or wrong way, only our own way that works best for us.

When you start journaling, make sure to capture and articulate your mindset at the beginning. The younger people I mentor often ask me, "what would you tell yourself at my age?" Which is a tough question to answer because being a couple of decades removed from my early twenties and having no true documented reference point of my mindset, I only have a general idea. The best assessment I have is that I don't think I would have listened to an older version of myself because I wasn't actually looking for wisdom, and nothing would have sunk in.

Journaling, however, gives us these detailed glimpses into moments of time in our lives. What we're hoping for, what we're working on, and our perspective on life.

This becomes valuable in at least two ways. One, it becomes a record and evidence of our intentionality about growth. Far too often, when we find ourselves in a place in our life that is low or difficult, it is easy to be too hard on ourselves. When we begin to value the effort not the outcome, we can look back and see how long we have been putting in the work. This should fuel our confidence to keep on pushing towards our goals.

Second, it helps force our brain to unpack what is really happening in life. Again, when things aren't going the way we wanted, it is easy for our brain to fixate on all the things that are wrong, or we are eager to seek out blame, which often lands back upon ourselves. This only keeps us in a negative, stagnant mind state for longer. By being intentional and working to get our thoughts onto paper in detail, we can begin to get better at exercising more control over our thought patterns.

If nothing else, keeping some type of journal is very therapeutic. We need to not only remove the stigma of going through therapy but also make it a standard to go.

I find it strange that despite the fact there's no user manual for successfully working on a human brain, and in an increasingly complicated world, we have held a stigma about seeking professional help for many years. Only recently have we started to bring conversations about mental help into the mainstream.

Statistically, we know that most people globally are going through some issues. Recent studies suggest that one in four adults in America are dealing with anxiety or depression. Whether this is dealing with something in the now, issues from our past, or the challenges that come from relationships in our lives, all of it adds up and makes it even more difficult to enjoy our lives to the fullest.

One of the biggest benefits that professional therapeutic services help us is by getting things out from within the recesses of our minds and into a space where we can work through and on them.

When we try and tackle things from within our own mind alone, we almost always are going to lose the battle. Journaling should allow you a space to get it out and reflect on what has been bouncing around inside your head.

I don't want to oversimplify what therapists do, but this at the core of how they help; they extract.

Of course, their ability in what to do with the stuff that comes out is where they've studied and trained to supply support. The premise is still that part of the process is extraction, reflection, resolution or work. The same way our journaling should work.

Estimate for a moment all the lifetime experiences you've had: the memories, and all the things tucked away in your subconscious. There's a lot of little pieces. A lot of popular science will tell you there is a distinct difference in your mental abilities being in a cluttered environment compared to clean and organized one.

Think about that, then combine that with the fact that our brains are designed to only take in and focus upon a fraction of all the billions of pieces of information all around us at any given moment. The opportunity for mental clutter is everywhere. Journaling provides a space to unpack, declutter and reorganize our thinking.

How and when are we ever shown how to do this, let alone the benefits of it? We've all met people whose minds seem to be unorganized and scattered. They always seem to be just catching up, and skating by rather than intentionally taking on tasks and life's events.

Each of us in the absence of intentionally organizing all this data from our lifetime of experiences, are leaving optimized thinking and clarity on the table.

Ultimately, learning to effectively journal in the way that works best for us, can help fuel our confidence as we navigate our way into the future. If you were to rate your life today, holistically on a scale of 1-10, based on where you are currently in comparison to where you want to be; then you committed to updating your progress at whatever frequency (at minimum a few times a month) and did a reevaluation quarterly – think about what that clarity would give you.

Journaling and journaling effectively for *you* gives you a base to intentionally move your life, and your goals toward the future you have designed.

MILE MARKERS

If someone were to stop you on the street and ask, "what are five wins you had over the last few months?" How ready would you be to answer?

If you are like most people, and I ask people this question a lot, you may struggle to name five specific wins in the last couple of months.

A big reason for this is that we live in what I like to call a "Superbowl" society, where we tend to only celebrate wins if they are big ones.

However, to get to a Superbowl, there's hundreds of smaller, but necessary wins that have to happen.

We should be naming wins every day. Did you wake up this morning? Win. Over 100,000 people who woke up yesterday, didn't wake up today. See it as a win. Did you have the opportunity or the ability to choose what you ate today? Win. With a significant portion of the world's population unable to say the same, you are winning. Do you have at least one person or thing in your life that brings a smile to your face? Win. One in four people, that's 25% are struggling with depression and anxiety. Having someone we care about, or who cares about us, or having something that brings us joy – no matter how simple or small, is a win.

I assume by now you get the point. However, this will give us zero benefit if we don't take the time to truly recognize and call out these wins. I push back against the notion of "small wins." A win is a win. What many people would call a small win, I call momentum. The law of momentum is one of the most powerful forces on earth, but if we're not calling out, recognizing and extracting the benefits of these wins, large or "small," then they aren't fueling our momentum.

It doesn't take much to know that trials and tribulations are a part of life and will undoubtedly occur in our lives. Can we try to minimize them? Of course, and we should do what we can to avoid unnecessary negativity, risk, or trouble when possible. However, many people run from challenges to the point that they avoid taking necessary action at all and settle into a less than optimal life. In the name of staying comfortable or avoiding something, they have left potential and opportunity on the table. Stepping into our future with confidence is easier when we know and can see that we have momentum.

Think about how momentum plays a role in sports. There is a reason they talk about it during games, while it's happening because there is clear and present impact it has on the game.

One of the best examples I've seen of this is can be seen in college basketball. Think about what you see when a team has "momentum." Their body language is different. Their language to each other is elevated. There is a clear and present difference in their overall demeanor, and everyone can see it. It is noticed and talked about by the announcers. It has an impact on the game.

The question is, did that momentum just start and happen in the game? No! It is the result of practice and preparation that helps fuel the team to be able to gain that confidence in the moment. A lot of this starts with how they are training their minds to face adversity when it shows up in the game. It shows up in how the coach approaches their readiness for the other team.

I love how legendary UCLA Men's basketball coach, John Wooden viewed this and constantly prepared his team. He spent very little time focused on the other team, worrying about what they might or might not do. Rather, he focused almost all of he and his players' attention on the things that were 100% in their control. This starts with our attitude and effort. From there we can effectively or ineffectively handle adversity. It was this level of "controlled mind state" that allowed his players to remain mentally prepared regardless of the environments or the level of talent they were up against. It was this type of approach that helped Coach Wooden go down as the greatest college basketball coach of all time winning an astounding 10 national championships.

In this same way, how are we preparing for the moments of adversity in our life? Are we focused on what we can control and influence? This starts with counting and measuring the wins along the way. Coach Wooden knew if his teams were ready when they had really good practices. He was an extremely detailed man who had his practices designed with a high level of intention. It was the winning in those small parts of the practice that fueled what it took to have momentum and win in the big moments.

How can we take this same approach into our daily lives? It starts with noticing, naming, and feeling good about the number of wins we have every day, week and month. When we give individual moments this level of attention and focus, we will find ourselves winning a whole lot more. When you start to win more, it fuels your level of confidence. When your confidence is elevated, everything else gets elevated.

How can you begin to elevate how you track and measure your wins today?

Great distances seem shorter when there's something to track along the way.

Think for a moment what it was like the last time you went on a really long road trip. I live in Sioux Falls, South Dakota, and I have made the 5-hour drive across the state to the Black Hills several times. The drive isn't terrible, but it's also not great. Most of the drive isn't very scenic, in fact, it's very flat and plain (…which is probably why they call them the Great Plains). One thing, however, that makes the drive more bearable are the mile markers along the way.

In those moments where it seems like I have been driving forever, and my inner child asks, "are we there yet," it's the mile markers that give me a glimpse of perspective. When I hit mile marker 300 coming home from the Black Hills, I know that just another 100 miles and I will have hit my destination. I know all of the time spent behind the wheel is getting me closer to home.

This same mentality can help us in the pursuit of our goals and dreams. Simply taking note of our wins consistently, helps show clear and present progress, even if it's just one step closer towards that goal.

Mile markers can and should provide much needed accountability. As we talk about in one of our trainings "The PRO-CESS: Progress towards Success," wherever there is a lack of wins, it is always preceded by a lack of work.

> **Wherever there is a lack of WINS, it is always preceded by a lack of WORK.**
>
> THINK 3D

Where we find a lack of work, we must be honest whether we really want what we are pursuing. Success can be broken down into wants, work, and wins. The tracking and measurement of wins helps hold us accountable to consistently take some form of action towards the things we would say that we wanted.

At minimum, we should be doing some level of quarterly goal setting or even defining one thing we'd like to do over the next 1-3 months. We know that any given month can get away from us because life happens. Work can get crazy, kid's activities, going through an emotional relationship challenge, insert whatever you want, are all things that many people go through any given month. However, looking at our goals over a quarter makes it so much more practical and manageable. We have 2,160 hours in a 90-day window of time. That is a lot of time to justify not being able to take some level of considerable progress towards our goals or at least one thing that would improve our life.

Before we land the plane on mile markers, let's take this one level deeper.

Pretend it is one-year from today. You just had the best year of your life. What is one thing personally and one thing professionally that would have to be true for you to say that with confidence, it was indeed the best year of your life?

The first step to being able to answer this is being intimate and clear with what we really want. Second, we need to have a base line for what the best year, has looked like up until this point.

A barrier to this for many people, is that some wouldn't be able to pinpoint what year they'd be competing against to have an idea of what is considered their best year. Even more alarming, for some even the suggestion that having "a best year" seems impossible.

This often can lead people to come up with wild or unrealistic realities or conditions that are outside of their control, or that have little to no chance of happening. Then it becomes easier to just sit in whatever their normal, or "good-enough" reality is because having their best year ever, seems so out of touch.

What if, however, we gave this some genuine and serious thought? What would you come up with if you really dedicated some time to thinking about what needs to happen to make this upcoming year, your best one so far.

I've said it before and I'll say it again, "*nothing of significance happens without intention.*" When we couple intention with action and track our progress along the way at least every three months, we see measurable momentum. We know we're moving in the right direction. Momentum builds the more we move, we just have to get started.

I have given you some space at the end of this book to get you started so that whether it takes a full year or less to make it through all 52 "Power Thoughts," along the way you will see and celebrate wins, build momentum, and elevate your life.

8

YOU ARE YOUR GREATEST ASSET – INVEST LIKE IT

At this time in your life, what would you consider to be your greatest assets?

For most people it would be things like their home, property, or investments.

What did it take to grow those assets? Mostly likely figuring out at one point in time that it was important to make an investment, i.e., taking on a mortgage payment or selecting to invest a percentage of your income into some sort of retirement account. Thankfully, what makes these types of investments successful is the "set it and forget it" aspect of letting something grow on its own. If we had to figure out each paycheck how much to stash away into a 401k, most of us would have significantly less than we have today. This is primarily because there are almost always more attractive priorities or exciting things to spend on in the moment, especially with the ease of how we are a few taps away from instant gratification for most purchases. I am immensely thankful for systems like autopay or automatic deductions to future protect me, from current me.

Though most people think of their financial assets as their most important, they are finite and variable to a large degree. No matter how much you invest in the stock market, a home, or other "things," there always exists some uncertainty of the return and the limited amount of that return on your investment.

We've also got this grossly wrong within the world of business. Peter Drucker, one of the most widely-known and influential thinkers on management, talked about this, noting that the mindset of businesses reflected what was found on their balance sheet. People show up as an expense, while machinery or equipment shows up as assets.

No matter how much time, energy, effort we pour into machines, there is always a maximum output to what it can produce. With machines, technology or processes, we can continue to improve and become more efficient and grow in overall output, of course, but there is still a cap to what it's capable of.

People on the other hand truly are limitless. Prior to this shifting of mindsets, and advancement of businesses within the information age this was seldom, if ever, a consideration.

We know that the human mind is the most complex super-computer ever created. We are still in the beginning phases of really understanding the mind, yet the undeniable reality is no one has come close to defining the limit of what we're truly capable of.

Take Roger Bannister for example. Roger was the first man to break the 4-minute mile. Prior to doing so, even scientists were convinced that it was impossible for humans to achieve such a feat. Some even suggested that a person's heart could explode in the attempt.

Yet, on May 6th, 1954, Roger Bannister did the impossible by running the mile in 3 minutes and 59 seconds. Once this long held belief was broken open, it took just a mere 46 days later for someone to best this record. Stated again…

> **Man's mind, stretched to a new idea, never goes back to its original dimension.**
> OLIVER WENDELL HOLMES

As we look back over our lives, if we considered our mind to be an investment portfolio, what would our net worth be today? Revisiting the premise of why our homes and 401k's work so well, it is the consistent, set it and forget it part that makes them effective. However, outside of this, given our "free" time, there are a never-ending number of places to spend our time, energy, attention, and focus. However, if we are unable to clearly articulate and supply evidence of when and how we're investing into ourselves, we're either consciously or subconsciously saying other things are more important than what we truly want out of life.

Before we leave this thought, let's look at the evidence, for we live in a society of an overabundance of empty opinions. Think about the people that you admire the most in life. They could be those you know personally or people you know of who you look up to. When we begin to unpack their lives and what we admire about them, we most likely would label them successful based on our personal definition of success. We know that no one simply stumbles upon success, it is an outcome from intentional actions over a period of time. Those who are successful in their marriage, invested time into the relationship to get it to that place. Those who are successful in their careers, invested the time to cross that threshold of success as well. No matter what the context of which areas we view someone as successful in, a commonality we're sure to find is some level of intentional investment into themselves. When someone feels incomplete or inadequate, it completely stifles their ability to try at aspiring for more. However, those who despite whatever backgrounds they came from or obstacles they faced, with intentional and consistent investment into themselves, built a foundation from which they were able to launch themselves into success.

Looking at the lives of these individuals, how does that compare or stack up against the average we see around us? To be clear, average isn't an insult. By definition, average is the majority. But when we look at the behaviors, the levels of investment to personal and professional growth, and people's aspirations, there becomes a clear separation of how people arrive to where they are today.

The question we should regularly be asking of ourselves is, which one do we want to align ourselves with? Almost everyone would say they want better for themselves and their lives, but not until we truly view ourselves as our greatest asset and commit to pouring regular and consistent time into our minds, we will continue to get what we've always had.

DESIGNING OUR LIFE WITH INTENTION

You probably didn't know it when the movie came out, but *The Matrix,* had a profound and lasting impact on how we view, think, and talk about reality and society.

Think about how many people you see in the day-to-day, who seem to be living in "the matrix." Maybe even you feel like that at times - caught up in the rinse and repeat cycle, just going through life on autopilot, without a deeper sense of awareness. Not that it's all bad, but it's just "good enough."

Most people I talk to want a better life or want more from the life they are currently living, yet very few of those people are taking consistent, persistent steps towards creating that better life.

There's not enough room in this book for me to dive into all the ways that our brain is wired, but one of the simplest ways I can put it is – the brain is wired for comfort and survival.

The brain wants our bodies to stay comfortable and alive, this is why we store fat, this is why we are afraid of the dark, this is why most people have some fear of snakes, spiders, etc.

In our modern life, it looks like comfort. Comfort really is an addiction. Thousands of years ago being uncomfortable meant uncertainty. Uncertainty meant a much higher likelihood of not surviving. Given that the brains primary function is to survive and keep us alive, not necessarily achieving success and thriving, it is easy to see and understand how our brains were design to love the feeling of comfort.

In today's day and age, there are no longer saber-toothed tigers waiting to eat us or having the chances of an unknown plant killing us. The trouble is that our brains haven't evolved to realize that there is no longer this same need for the fear of the unknown that has served us well over the entire existence of the human species.

We still fear challenge, discomfort, and uncertainty the same way.

Early on in this book I posed the question that out of the hundreds and maybe thousands of people that you know, are there at least 5 individuals who are truly and genuinely living their best life? It is rare to get even a handful of people who can say this with confidence. This is an interesting realization, especially living in a country where we have the freedom to choose where we live, what we do for a living, the people we're around, and the things we engage with. We are a country that stands for the epitome of free will and personal freedom of CHOICE. So why are so many people, not choosing to think differently, act differently, or pursue their higher potential?

It's my opinion, and my experience, that in our own way, many of us are living in a matrix. Remember how many thoughts we have each day, most of them approximately the same as they were yesterday? (Hint if you skipped here without reading the beginning – it's about 60,000.)

So, if we think similarly to the environments we came from, the people we spend the most time around, and the thought patterns we have the most often – it becomes easier to see beyond the veil, and into the reality that many of us or the people we know are just "existing."

So how do we begin to break through? It starts with intention. *Nothing of significance happens without intention.* Don't miss the depth of truth in this statement. Most people generally understand this concept, but if they truly valued the reality behind it, they would be far more mindful of the moments that make up their lives and ask, "what level of intention am I bringing into this next chapter of my life?"

Pause for a moment and ask, "what was my intention in picking up this book to read it?"

More than likely, you know deep down you are capable of more. You have a desire to improve, for your life to get better, and to step into your **Higher Potential** with confidence.

Yet, you also know that there's a reason most New Year's resolutions fail, and that most people don't accomplish the goals they set out for themselves, you included. This time it needs to be different.

This time something HAS TO change.

The way around this is outlined a few different ways in this book. Simply put, you need to sit down and design. Take time to design the life, the outcome, the reality you want then take action, and start thinking about your life with intention. The consistent and persistent pursuit of elevating your thinking and acting with intention will elevate your life.

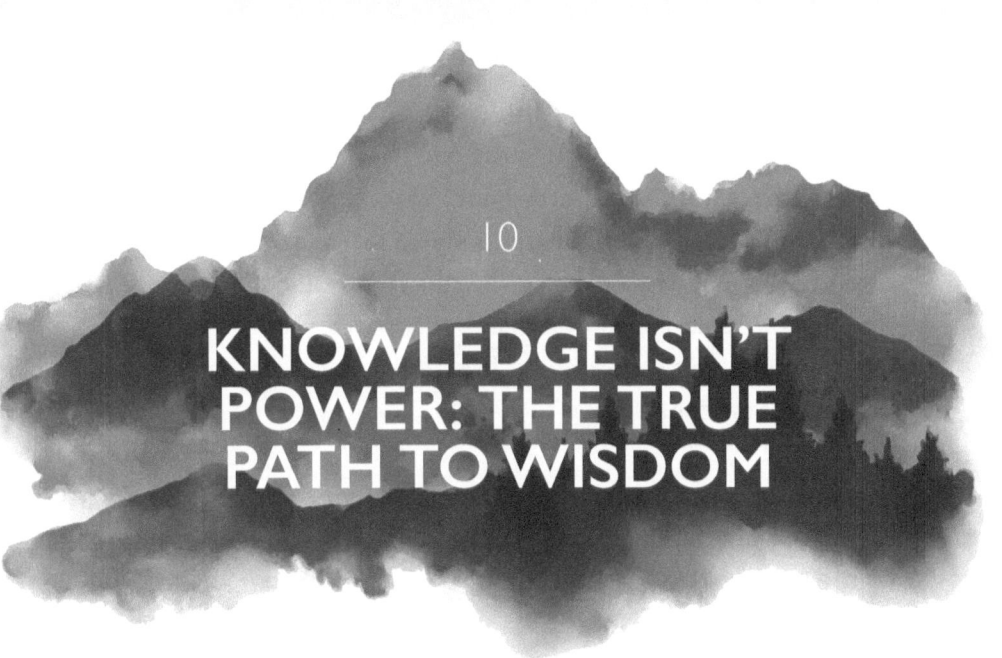

KNOWLEDGE ISN'T POWER: THE TRUE PATH TO WISDOM

It is confession time.

I am an information junkie and I have an addiction to new information. There I said it.

Now, odds are if you're a reader, listen to podcasts or audiobooks, you too are an information junkie. It is understandable to see why. Our brains love new information. New ways of thinking. It is the key of how our society has grown so quickly as we are leaping from the platforms of wisdoms from those who have come before us.

Here is the danger of being a junkie or addict – we always need more to get our fix. And in a time of endless information, where we can 3x speed those podcasts or audio books all we want, we will never get ALL the information.

For me, physical books are my drug of choice. There is nothing like cracking open that brand new book, with my yellow highlighter, just waiting for the new thoughts to be fed to me. Personally, I love the thought of gaining the insight from someone's hundreds of hours of thinking and experience on a subject boiled down into a few hundred pages of content. It is 100% one of the best returns on your investment ever!

You might be asking, if you agree there is so much benefit to gaining the insight and knowledge from others, wherein lies the problem? Pause here and ask yourself this question, how much of the things you learn do you actually put into practice?

My reality was that I was far more in love with the dating process of the information than settling down with it, engaging with it, or fully committing myself to it. Most sages of the past were passing along critical things that genuinely helped them excel in life that was only found after years of experience and testing out the truth behind what they were passing on. Yet, most people couldn't name 5 key pieces of wisdom they've married themselves to in the last few years.

I heard Bishop T.D. Jakes, one of the world's most revered masterminds, say once that it is true in life, we cannot do better if we don't know better - but all of us know better than we do. That resonated with me so deep in my soul I felt like he was counseling me right there in my car (as I was on a YouTube information binge).

Looking back on my growth and development, I could have been so much further in so many areas of my life if I had gotten this critical piece of advice earlier on. For the better part of 15 years, from my mid-twenties to early forties, I became obsessed with gaining knowledge. However, looking back, I couldn't confidently stand on what were those key things that I really sunk my teeth into.

Don't get me wrong, mere exposure to books, lessons, and knowledge, has been the most influential thing I have ever done. It has helped to elevate the way I think dramatically. But what I am aiming at is getting the most return on the investment of our time, energy, and effort.

Again, *nothing of significance happens without intention.*

We have all heard the saying that knowledge is power. However, I believe that most people fully realize that knowledge by itself isn't power. It is only applied knowledge that has power. And it is only experienced knowledge that turns into wisdom.

> *"Knowledge isn't power. Applied knowledge is power. And it is only experienced knowledge that turns into wisdom."*

I developed my process for how I engage with books from the person who had the most professional influence on my life, John C. Maxwell, world renown leadership author and guru. It was stumbling upon his books as a naive twenty something year old that change the trajectory of my life. In reading over 40 of his books, along with hundreds of others, early on I began wondering why it seemed his books were filled with so much good information. John reveals that he is an information collector. Whenever he reads something good, whether in a book or magazine, he has a filing system to retain that key information.

It was from this example that I began highlighting books and then writing those highlighting into notebooks to capture the key thoughts or ideas. In my now evolved process, I still date a lot of information, however I now spend prioritized time engaging with those few key things that I know will make me better and help evolve my perspective.

We can pass down knowledge to others, but if we aren't willing to go through the experience of that knowledge, we'll never gain the wisdom that it holds. Taking the time to unpack and apply it in our lives has the direct obvious benefit, but also becomes a living, breathing example of its application that others can benefit from.

Before leaving this chapter, ask yourself how can you elevate your own path of truly engaging and settling down with the knowledge available to us that can help us to transform our lives?

THE PATHWAY

Even though we have more information available to us today than any other point in history, which allows us to study the lives of anyone we see as successful, why do so few actually find the path for themselves?

Once again revisiting the 60,000 thoughts we have each day, what direction are our thoughts leading us?

Let's look at this another way...

How accountable do we hold ourselves for the outcome of our lives?

Of course, we know we have the freedom of choice in the moment, yet very few genuinely look at how we arrived at certain points in our life or how particular events unfolded Part of the reason few people do so is the way our brains are wired. They act like a safety mechanism to help prevent us from beating ourselves up as many people have the tendency to do.

The goal of doing a thorough evaluation of responsibility for the outcomes of our lives has extraordinarily little to do with placing blame on anyone, including ourselves, but finding the root cause with the purpose and intent of better informing us going forward.

Think back for a moment to some key experiences in your life. What would happen if someone wouldn't have treated you the way that they did or said that thing to you?

Often, I hear stories of people discussing an influential person in their life who was potentially a coach, teacher, or a boss, and their simple belief in that person in the right moment gave them not only confidence in that moment but carried them for several years changing the trajectory of their life. On the other hand, I recently heard someone recalling what one kid said to them at church camp and how it affected them to where they still feel like they must prove that person wrong to this day.

When given the right space to understand the power of a moment, we know how powerful or detrimental the right or wrong moment can be on our lives. The point here is that the number one predictor of the outcomes in our lives is the actions that we take.

This makes our actions all the more important when we consider how we are exercising intention and elevated thinking. In the grand scheme of things, you can only control so much, in fact it's not much at all. The one thing you can control, is *you.*

Most of us would agree with the idea that as individuals we are responsible for our actions, but how many of us put real, purposeful intent into our daily actions with the specific focus of creating the outcomes or life we desire?

If we're measuring based off results, the answer is pretty low.

Repeating this once again because it truly is that important to etch into our brains, one of the foundational beliefs at Think 3D is the idea that *nothing of significance happens without intention.* When we unpack our calendars, all the days, weeks and months; how much of our time is truly spent *intentionally?*

For most of us, as we have already covered, we get swept up in "busy" and rely on the autopilot of our routines, without consideration to adjusting our environment or exposure and how they impact our actions and outcomes.

When we get honest about where we are spending our precious time, we all have much more control over it than we hold ourselves accountable to.

One of the silver linings of going through the COVID pandemic was that it slowed the world down and showed us we didn't *have* to be this busy. It was a rude awakening for many who otherwise ran on cruise control and didn't realize the toll it was taking on them, their family or their health.

The unfortunate reality coming out on the other side of the pandemic is that most people did not take lasting advantage of the perspective gained while they had the time to reevaluate what they wanted their life to look like going forward.

Once things got back to "normal," most found themselves swept right back up to the busyness of the world and jumped back into the same routine without a significant change.

The question I want to challenge us all with is this, if we know that our actions are the number one predictor of our outcomes, how can we begin to take more *intentional* actions toward creating the elevated life we want?

It comes down to a choice. The question remains, will we make it a priority to do something different or keep getting caught up in "busy" as much of the world continues to do?

Let's take a minute to pause and unpack our actions more.

What is the number one predictor of our actions? It is our emotions. Think for a moment about the person who wants to get into shape for themselves. They are very clear that the actions required are to get up in the morning and go work out at the gym. They set their intention. They know why they want it, for the outcome of feeling and looking good. Then the alarm goes off at 5am… they hit snooze several times over until the thought goes through their head, "I'll start tomorrow."

Now, we all have been there in some way or another. We've all experienced the greatest impediments to today's success – "tomorrow." In this example, we are clear on our outcomes and the actions needed, but in the moment, we didn't "feel" like it.

On the other hand, the person who chooses to get up every day and does indeed get their butt into the gym, they did so because they "felt" enough motivation to get them going.

Many studies suggest that around 40% of our lives are driven by habits and routines. However, the key things required to get us to the point of developing the habit, take willpower and mental exertion to get us into action. As we all know too well, how we "feel" in the moment is extremely powerful.

Take time as you continue to grow in this process and elevate your thinking, unpack the actions you take or don't take on a daily basis and identify the emotions you experience prior to making a move.

"Why didn't you go to work today?" "Because I didn't *feel* like it."

"Why did you yell at your kids like that?" "Because I *felt* frustrated and angry."

"Wow, you developed your whole business plan over the weekend!" "Yeah, I *felt* really inspired."

There are a ton of amazing books and resources that go into the science of how our brains and emotions drive us to action, often at a subconscious level. However, for the sake of keeping this simple – your emotions are the primary driver of your actions, or lack of them.

Now I want to go one layer deeper. What is the number one indicator of our emotions? Our thoughts. Let's unpack this the same way.

Think back to the last time you felt angry, what were you thinking about? How about the last time you felt inspired? What were you thinking about? If you go through your most common emotional states and unpack what it is you were thinking about when you were happy, sad, frustrated, etc., what do you find?

What you think about, creates the emotions you feel. The emotions you feel drive your actions. The actions you take create the outcome of your life. All of this can be traced back to your thoughts, and how you think.

Our lives become what we think about most often. This has been repeated and proven time and time again, either for better or for worse – our lives are driven by our thoughts.

The good news is that this realization points us back to where our power truly lies – in the moment.

Most people fail to take control of their lives because they've been swept up in mimicking the world around them and end up settling for the best version of a lesser life. I would challenge you to pause and really evaluate the world around you and notice how most people have settled for "good enough." The saying "it could be worse" makes my skin crawl. It's redundant and it's something that always goes without saying. Yet, for some reason, just because things *could* be worse, so many people settle for whatever life gives to them. It's limiting, because the reality is, just saying "it could be worse," and accepting whatever life happens to throw at you, absolves you of the responsibility of changing things that *are* in your control – primarily the way you think.

Yes, life in the macro or large-scale, can be complicated and overwhelming with the challenges we face, different things pulling for our attention, and our history or hard-wired ways of thinking. However, life in the micro, life in this moment, is manageable. In small moments, individual thoughts and actions, we have a decision to make. Are we going to choose to aim our intentions, thoughts, emotions and actions in the direction we say we want to go?

HOW TO GET THE MOST
OUT OF THIS TOOL

Before you get into the part of this book that is designed to help elevate your thinking, and elevate your life, I want you to answer this question:

Are you *committed* to improving your life, or simply interested?

If you've made it to this point of the book, you are at least interested in growing and evolving into that next version of you.

However, being *interested* or just wanting something isn't enough. There's a reason the diet and exercise industry are a multi-billion-dollar beast, built on the foundation of people looking for hacks, short cuts, and easy ways to get what they want.

The reality is there is no "silver-bullet." There is no quick trip to the next best version of ourselves.

Everything I've written in this entire book is simple – it's far from rocket science. However, simple doesn't mean it's *easy.* Like I said, we are hard-wired beings, our brains care for, and push us towards familiarity. The path to elevated thinking and an elevated life requires real, genuine commitment.

This is the entire point of "Power Thoughts." If you elevate your thinking, you can elevate your life. Whether you are reading this to take the next step in your career, or you are seeking to grow personally and in your home life – the one thing you can expect is to have to push through and stay consistent when you don't feel like it.

I will tell you from personal experience, success lies on the other side of "I don't feel like it."

> ### Success lies on the other side of "I don't feel like it."
> TAMIEN DYSART, THINK 3D

So, get clear and get intimate with the vision of what the "other side" looks and feels like. What will a better you mean?

Personally – Think about all the people in your life that will benefit from an elevated version of you. How would that make you feel, knowing you were making a significant difference simply based on your example? How about by what you share with others who are ready to grow to in their lives? What would it mean to blaze a trail of possibilities and genuinely live your best life knowing that your kids, future kids, or the next generation behind you saw a new world of possibilities simply by watching your accomplishments?

Professionally – In a world where most people stop intentionally growing, developing, and learning beyond their school years, what would that do for you as you continue to evolve into a better version of yourself professionally? You can start simple – identify the key characteristics or competencies of the leaders you admire most, then rate yourself 1-10 on those things.

From there, you have a clear and simple, yet impactful list of things you can work towards to step into becoming a better leader for the rest of your career.

Elevating our thinking is universally beneficial, it will change every area of your life and therefore should be placed where it belongs, high up on our priority list. Where have you decided to place it on your life?

DEVELOPING A WINNER'S MINDSET

Let's do a quick pulse check of society. Sometime in the next few days, ask as many people as you'd like this simple question: What are 3 wins you've had in the last 3 months?

Like I said earlier, what you're most likely to find is that the many people struggle to name just 3 wins in the last 3 months.

The new car effect happens when we buy a new car, the very next day we now notice dozens of cars that look just like ours on the road. Once our brains become aware of something, it notices it everywhere. The basic idea of looking for, noticing, naming, and calling out your wins will begin to shift your mindset, and you will see them more often.

Think about what happens when you name wins every day.

Once you notice and feel like you're winning every day, what does that make you? A winner! The power of wins transforms your perspective, and you begin to see yourself and your life differently. I have seen this simple mind-shift transform all kinds of individuals once they realized that for most of their life, their perspective wasn't focused on wins. When you feel like a winner, you start acting like a winner.

There are several benefits to our lives holistically when we feel like a winner, but I want to call out a few quick ones at the top of my list. When you feel like a winner, it helps boost your confidence and happiness. These are two words that should be on everyone's definition of success. Think for a moment, is there any area of your life that wouldn't benefit the more confident and happier you are? Of course not. Therefore, simply by calling out wins on a regular basis, you will begin to add to and fuel these key characteristic traits that has universal benefit in every area of our lives.

I created space at the end of this book so you can begin to track your wins and look back over the course of engaging with this process to see the amount of wins you begin to pile up along your journey of elevating your thinking and elevating your life. Challenge yourself to engage in noticing, naming, becoming more aware of and tracking your wins on a daily or weekly basis, and see how much you can do.

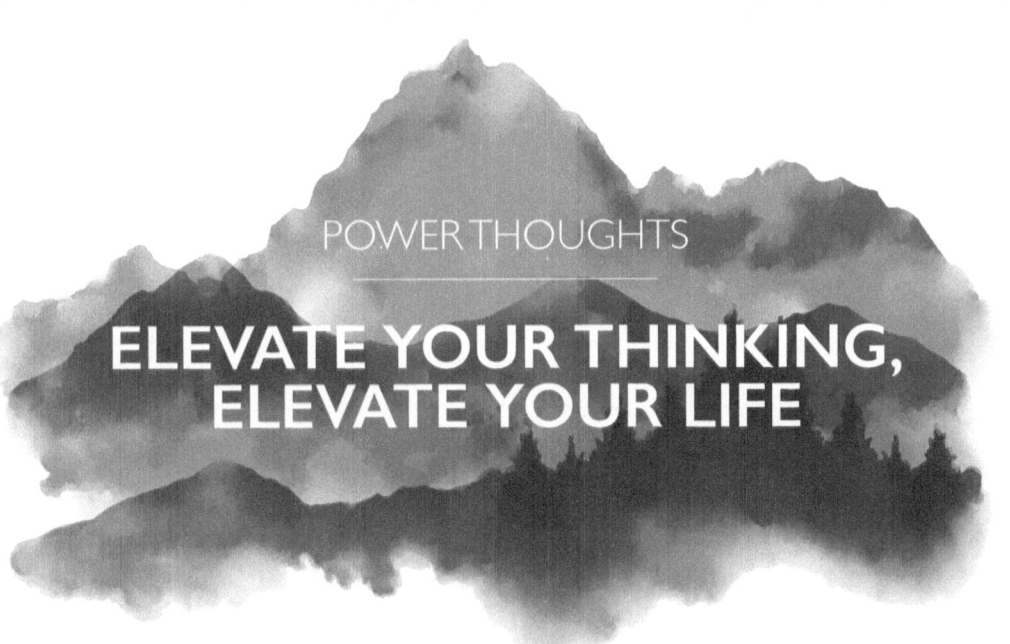

POWER THOUGHTS

ELEVATE YOUR THINKING, ELEVATE YOUR LIFE

What to expect from Power Thoughts

Use these weekly checkpoints to soak something in from the quotes, and work through the questions and commit at least 15-20 minutes every week to intentionally elevating your thoughts around these topics.

The second piece will be to commit to taking action to get one step closer to the future and the life you want to achieve, through unlocking more of your potential.

These are designed to be taken slow, and intentionally, so make sure to carve out time each week.

You may recall from earlier in our book, I challenged you to find an accountability partner, or a source of weekly accountability from a friend. Now is the time to start that. Every week make sure you are taking 20 minutes at least, to better yourself, to check in, to journal and to grow.

Everything I have shared along the way has been to get your mind primed and ready to embark on this process of self-discovery, growth, and elevation.

Remember – a rising tide lifts all boats.

ONE

Everything can be taken from a man but one thing; the last of human freedoms – to choose one's attitude in any given set of circumstances, to choose one's own way.

Victor Frankl

How much are you exercising your freedom to choose the kind of life you want?

It is an unfortunate thing to see that most of society has absolved themselves of the freedom to live the life they want by defaulting to "this is just the way things are!"

The reality of this is that once people get to a place of awareness that a better life may be possible, they think it is impossible to get there because they have allowed themselves to get cornered into a life that was not designed with intention and thus not an easy thing to turn around.

Let's be clear, the path to living our best life isn't an easy one, but it should be worth it. As Les Brown, the great motivational speaker said, "If we do what is easy, life will be hard. But if we do what is hard, life will be easy." I would add to that by saying a life that we genuinely enjoy living.

If Victor Frankl could find it in himself to choose his attitude in the unimaginable circumstances of surviving through Nazi Germany death camps, I would have to believe that whatever we may be dealing with in life isn't severe enough to justify that we too can't choose a right attitude.

How and where can we begin to choose an intentional attitude as we look to improve the trajectory of our life?

What did you soak in from this Power Thought?

What are you going to do to engage with this thought, challenge or topic throughout the week?

ELEVATE

Make time to document your thoughts, and what you are observing around this topic or challenge. Remember journaling is for *you*, what you need to extract, document, apply, and grow.

☐ Check this box when you have taken and completed
one action towards this topic.

Are you more addicted to the idea or the implementation?
Your Power Thoughts are an investment into your future self.

_____

_____

_____

_____

_____

_____

_____

_____

_____

_____

Two

For I have always maintained that, excepting fools, men do not differ much in intellect, only in zeal and hard work: and I still think this is an eminently important difference.

Charles Darwin

How would you differentiate yourself from those people who are content living an average life?

For most people, when they are on the side of the "have not's," it is the easy assumption that they aren't as smart as the successful entrepreneur or the lawyer. However, as many people find out along their career path, most people we meet along the way really aren't any smarter than we are.

When it really comes down to it, it is passion, zeal, and hard work that becomes the true great separator of the successful. All things that are available to all of us.

How could you evaluate and measure these critical areas and follow-up to increase them?

What did you soak in from this Power Thought?

What are you going to do to engage with this thought, challenge or topic throughout the week?

ELEVATE

Make time to document your thoughts, and what you are observing around this topic or challenge. Remember journaling is for *you*, what you need to extract, document, apply, and grow.

☐ Check this box when you have taken and completed *one action towards this topic.*

Are you more addicted to the idea or the implementation? Your Power Thoughts are an investment into your future self.

_____

_____

_____

_____

_____

_____

_____

_____

_____

_____

THREE

Be grateful for all that you have, accept all that you don't,
and actively create all that you want.

Hal Elrod

Given your current reality, how content are you? Truly?

Isn't it interesting that most people will justify that they are happy with where they are in life at the current moment yet are far from "living their BEST life?"

Deeply rooted in our survival instincts is the need or desire to not feel bad, therefore this justification that life is "good enough" is simply a defense mechanism.

Given that we are indeed the captains of our ship, either intentionally steering it or defaulting to drift aimlessly, shouldn't we ensure we're targeting a course to make the journey as enjoyable as possible? Of course!

A great starting place is grounding ourselves in gratitude, not placing blame for what isn't but accepting reality for what it is now and working toward the things we want for our future.

How can you begin to improve upon all 3 of these areas?

What did you soak in from this Power Thought?

What are you going to do to engage with this thought, challenge or topic throughout the week?

ELEVATE

Make time to document your thoughts, and what you are observing around this topic or challenge. Remember journaling is for *you*, what you need to extract, document, apply, and grow.

☐ Check this box when you have taken and completed *one action towards this topic.*

Are you more addicted to the idea or the implementation?
Your Power Thoughts are an investment into your future self.

_____

_____

_____

_____

_____

_____

_____

_____

_____

_____

FOUR

There is no way to happiness – happiness is the way.
Thich Nhat Hanh

On a scale of 1-10, where would you rate your overall happiness in your life right now?

What would it take to improve this?

For most of our lives, we are taught (mostly unintentionally) that happiness is found externally. We will be happy when we get that certain job, going on vacation, or have a better relationship.

Though these things may be contributing factors to happiness, the true path to happiness is found on the road inward. Most people never find this path because we don't see it being modeled in abundance in society and instead continue to promote these temporary fixes to happiness.

As you march down this path of true inward satisfaction and happiness, let us keep in our sights that happiness is an emotion which is preceded by what we're thinking about. The more we focus upon what is already right with life and that happiness is far more perspective than obtainment, we will increasingly find ourselves enjoying life in each moment.

How can you continue to discover deeper levels of joy, contentment, and happiness on your journey?

What did you soak in from this Power Thought?

What are you going to do to engage with this thought, challenge or topic throughout the week?

ELEVATE

Make time to document your thoughts, and what you are observing around this topic or challenge. Remember journaling is for *you*, what you need to extract, document, apply, and grow.

☐ Check this box when you have taken and completed
   one action towards this topic.

Are you more addicted to the idea or the implementation?
Your Power Thoughts are an investment into your future self.

_____

_____

_____

_____

_____

_____

_____

_____

_____

_____

FIVE

Your level of success will rarely exceed your level of personal development because success is something you attract by the person you become.

Jim Rohn

How would you rate your current commitment toward personal development?

(Rate on a scale of 1-10, or describe your commitment in terms like "very committed," "somewhat committed," etc.)

What actions are you taking that confirm this level of commitment?

Not on a level of what you want to tell yourself or convince others of. On the level of evidence based. If you were in a court of law, what evidence would you bring forth to support your conviction of commitment?

We know that we all have more potential inside of us than we're actively pursuing.

In what ways and what areas could you turn up your level of personal development just one notch and step into your Higher Potential? Will you follow through?

What did you soak in from this Power Thought?

What are you going to do to engage with this thought, challenge or topic throughout the week?

ELEVATE

Make time to document your thoughts, and what you are observing around this topic or challenge. Remember journaling is for *you,* what you need to extract, document, apply, and grow.

☐ Check this box when you have taken and completed *one action towards this topic.*

Are you more addicted to the idea or the implementation?
Your Power Thoughts are an investment into your future self.

_____

_____

_____

_____

_____

_____

_____

_____

_____

_____

Six

It's about me rising to serve a mission, not the mission bowing down to match my limited strengths.

Unknown

Are you answering the call?

As we continue to go down the path of self-discovery and identify the things, we want most in life, are we courageously leaning into the obstacles between us and success?

Our brains really could care less about our goals and ambitions, but rather, are wired for comfort simply because comfort has meant survival for most of human existence.

However, today, especially with social media driving the comparison game, this comfort is at the core of most people's discontentment. They know deep down that more is possible and the constant exposure to what other people have reminds them they aren't where they'd like to be.

Where this goes wrong is when this leads them down a path of seeking happiness in the external environment. The real truth is the path toward our calling can only be found going within.

How can we take an honest look at what we need to do and ensure we're actively stepping into our purpose in life, which is tethered to our higher potential?

What did you soak in from this Power Thought?

What are you going to do to engage with this thought, challenge or topic throughout the week?

ELEVATE

Make time to document your thoughts, and what you are observing around this topic or challenge. Remember journaling is for *you*, what you need to extract, document, apply, and grow.

☐ Check this box when you have taken and completed *one action towards this topic.*

Are you more addicted to the idea or the implementation?
Your Power Thoughts are an investment into your future self.

_____

_____

_____

_____

_____

_____

_____

_____

_____

SEVEN

Ecstasy is a full, deep involvement in life.
John Lovell

How would you describe your engagement or relationship with life?

Take a moment and think back over your top 10-20 most enjoyable experiences in life. Odds are that almost all of them you were deeply engaged in an activity, enjoying life, and had others you care about sharing that experience with you.

Let us not simply leave these golden moments to just a handful of times throughout the year. Let us engage daily living with passion and intention.

It is along this path that one finds true joy. Once we truly understand that a great life is about the journey, not simply the destination, we should have an elevated aim going into each new week.

How can you be more present in everyday living and your activities to involve yourself truly and deeply in life, ongoingly stepping into your Higher Potential?

What did you soak in from this Power Thought?

What are you going to do to engage with this thought, challenge or topic throughout the week?

ELEVATE

Make time to document your thoughts, and what you are observing around this topic or challenge. Remember journaling is for *you*, what you need to extract, document, apply, and grow.

☐ Check this box when you have taken and completed *one action towards this topic.*

Are you more addicted to the idea or the implementation?
Your Power Thoughts are an investment into your future self.

_____

_____

_____

_____

_____

_____

_____

_____

_____

_____

EIGHT

Things do not necessarily happen for the best, but some people are able to make the best out of things that happened.

Tal Ben-Shahar

What is your current process for "growing through" your experiences in life?

Isn't it interesting that everyone knows absolutely that life comes with both ups and downs, peaks and valleys, yet the majority are most often caught unprepared for circumstances when they come and even worse, they leave learning from the challenging moments of life to chance.

As you examine the last few challenging moments in your life, how have you grown from them? Could you elevate and extract even greater value of the lessons being offered through them? How could you better prepare to optimize what you learn from future experiences?

The better prepared to learn from the tests of life, the sooner we'll be ready to graduate to those next levels of living.

What did you soak in from this Power Thought?

What are you going to do to engage with this thought, challenge or topic throughout the week?

ELEVATE

Make time to document your thoughts, and what you are observing around this topic or challenge. Remember journaling is for *you*, what you need to extract, document, apply, and grow.

☐ Check this box when you have taken and completed *one action towards this topic.*

**Are you more addicted to the idea or the implementation?
Your Power Thoughts are an investment into your future self.**

_____

_____

_____

_____

_____

_____

_____

_____

_____

NINE

Small minds talk about people. Average minds talk about events. Great minds talk about ideas.

Eleanor Roosevelt

What does the content of your conversations consist of?

For most people, it is a mixture of these things mentioned in this quote. However, we can see the general truism in this statement.

As we ask ourselves where it is we want to go in life, we quickly realize the importance of spending much more time engaging in the ideas necessary to get us from here to wherever "there" is.

How can you begin to redistribute the energy and content of your dialogue with others into more meaningful buckets and in doing so, think through those next right steps needed to elevate your life?

What did you soak in from this Power Thought?

What are you going to do to engage with this thought, challenge or topic throughout the week?

ELEVATE

Make time to document your thoughts, and what you are observing around this topic or challenge. Remember journaling is for *you*, what you need to extract, document, apply, and grow.

☐ Check this box when you have taken and completed *one action towards this topic.*

Are you more addicted to the idea or the implementation? Your Power Thoughts are an investment into your future self.

_____

_____

_____

_____

_____

_____

_____

_____

_____

_____

TEN

The best years of your life are the ones in which you decide your problems are your own. You do not blame them on your mother, the economy, or the president. You realize that you control your own destiny.

Bob Proctor

What good has blame done for you in your lifetime?

Reflecting back for a moment, let us recognize what blame is used for most of the time - to absolve ourselves of personal responsibility.

Knowing that the answer to the first question about blame, if it doesn't serve us, then why would we ever engage in it?

Even in moments where someone else may truly be at fault, it still is of a higher benefit to turn inward and ask what can I learn from this and/or look for any way to improve things within your sphere of control/influence going forward?

If we truly are to live a life of happiness and joy, it will require the highest level of personal responsibility. On this path, there is no use for blame but rather engaging in extreme ownership.

How can you take even more control over your destiny and the outcomes of your life?

What did you soak in from this Power Thought?

What are you going to do to engage with this thought, challenge or topic throughout the week?

ELEVATE

Make time to document your thoughts, and what you are observing around this topic or challenge. Remember journaling is for *you*, what you need to extract, document, apply, and grow.

☐ Check this box when you have taken and completed *one action towards this topic.*

Are you more addicted to the idea or the implementation?
Your Power Thoughts are an investment into your future self.

_____

_____

_____

_____

_____

_____

_____

_____

_____

_____

ELEVEN

The main thing is that greatness is doable. Greatness is many, many individual feats, and each of them is doable.

Dan Chambliss

How many people do you know, or have you encountered that truly aspire for greatness on a continual basis? For most, it is a rarity to come across these individuals, and when they do, it is clearly evident of their ambitions.

Why do you suppose more people don't?

For many or probably most, it is because greatness simply sounds too far or is too hard to achieve. But what if you were challenged simply to lock in on what greatness looked like today? Is that a possibility? Then what if you attempted for that daily greatness again and again, giving each day a new run of energy at just being great that day?

What we would find is that our weeks and months would start to gain more momentum. Working toward this momentum is one of the most powerful daily activities we can and should be engaging in.

What one would quickly realize is that greatness basically comes down to the CHOICE to be great. From this simple decision and perspective, greatness becomes doable.

How committed are you toward reaching for greatness and how could you raise it up just one notch from where it is today?

What did you soak in from this Power Thought?

What are you going to do to engage with this thought, challenge or topic throughout the week?

ELEVATE

Make time to document your thoughts, and what you are observing around this topic or challenge. Remember journaling is for *you*, what you need to extract, document, apply, and grow.

☐ Check this box when you have taken and completed *one action towards this topic.*

Are you more addicted to the idea or the implementation?
Your Power Thoughts are an investment into your future self.

_____

_____

_____

_____

_____

_____

_____

_____

_____

_____

TWELVE

Life isn't about wishing you were somewhere or someone that you're not. Life is about enjoying where you are, loving who you are, and consistently improving both.

Hal Elrod

At current, how much would you say you "love your life?"

Let's take this an honest layer deeper. If someone were to follow you around from 10 feet away for a week, would they agree with you on your assessment of how much you love your life?

It is unfortunate how much social media has influenced the comparisons we make both consciously and subconsciously.

Knowing that social media isn't going to have less of an influence on the future, how can we instead help to fortify ourselves to truly design and live our lives with intention based on our highest and truest desires?

Regardless of where you are at currently in life, how can you begin to enjoy being here right now, love yourself more, and work at elevating both consistently?

At the core of being human is the need/desire for progress. As we steadily work to see and experience progress in these areas, let this fuel our knowing that we are truly on our own unique path of living "our" best life.

What did you soak in from this Power Thought?

What are you going to do to engage with this thought, challenge or topic throughout the week?

ELEVATE

Make time to document your thoughts, and what you are observing around this topic or challenge. Remember journaling is for *you*, what you need to extract, document, apply, and grow.

☐ Check this box when you have taken and completed *one action towards this topic.*

Are you more addicted to the idea or the implementation?
Your Power Thoughts are an investment into your future self.

_____

_____

_____

_____

_____

_____

_____

_____

_____

_____

THIRTEEN

Action may not always bring happiness, but there is no happiness without action.

Benjamin Disraeli

How much control have you taken over your own happiness?

It is amazing how much people expect others to act in a certain way for them to be happy and content with their lives. Yet, how well has that EVER worked out?

A truly happy life is one worth working towards.

Happiness doesn't just fall into our laps. The real question is, are we really willing to put forth the effort necessary to live a genuinely happy life?

Given that every part of life is better and more positively impacted from a vantage point of happiness, let us indeed DECIDE to go all in to live and be happy.

How can you elevate your actions steps toward your next level of happiness and satisfaction in life?

What did you soak in from this Power Thought?

What are you going to do to engage with this thought, challenge or topic throughout the week?

ELEVATE

Make time to document your thoughts, and what you are observing around this topic or challenge. Remember journaling is for *you*, what you need to extract, document, apply, and grow.

☐ Check this box when you have taken and completed *one action towards this topic.*

Are you more addicted to the idea or the implementation?
Your Power Thoughts are an investment into your future self.

_____

_____

_____

_____

_____

_____

_____

_____

_____

_____

FOURTEEN

Human excellence is a state of mind.

Socrates

As you look back over the last 7 days, what states of mind would you describe yourself to be in most of the time?

As we abstractedly evaluate the various mind states we find ourselves in, how many of them are with intention and how may are a mere default based on the environment, circumstances, or those we're engaging with?

At its core, excellence is a CHOICE. We can CHOOSE to wake up with an attitude and commitment to live excellent, do excellent work, and view the world in an excellent way.

The other option is to allow ourselves to wander into our days and at best, simply "hope" for the best.

Simply because why would we choose not to, how can we DECIDE on a more frequent basis to put our mind state at a level of excellence as we step into our **Higher Potential** and daily aspiration to be the best we can in that moment?

What did you soak in from this Power Thought?

What are you going to do to engage with this thought, challenge or topic throughout the week?

ELEVATE

Make time to document your thoughts, and what you are observing around this topic or challenge. Remember journaling is for *you*, what you need to extract, document, apply, and grow.

☐ Check this box when you have taken and completed *one action towards this topic.*

Are you more addicted to the idea or the implementation?
Your Power Thoughts are an investment into your future self.

_____

_____

_____

_____

_____

_____

_____

_____

_____

_____

FIFTEEN

You should never be satisfied. Happy, but not satisfied.
Dissatisfaction is a creative state. It took you out of the
cave and put you into the condominium. It gave you the
wheel, the fax, and the furnace. Dissatisfaction gave you
and me a lifestyle that is the envy of the world. Develop a
healthy dissatisfaction with your life. Set new goals, big,
exciting goals. Then, set out to achieve them with the same
enthusiasm as a youthful toddler. That is called living.
Everything else is dying.

Bob Proctor

Where do you currently have dissatisfaction at in your life?

It is amazing how contrary society wants to view and approach this vantage point around dissatisfaction. Yet, most of the world isn't genuinely happy, rather addicted to "good enough" and are leaving their goals/aspirations for their dreams - only the kind when we're sleeping.

What does it mean to you to truly be "ALIVE!"?

In our inner honesty, we know there is no easy street to our highest level of satisfaction in life. Let us not just be okay with the view on dissatisfaction but embrace it to leverage the fuel it gives us.

How can you begin to close the gaps around one area of dissatisfaction as you step into your Higher Potential?

What did you soak in from this Power Thought?

What are you going to do to engage with this thought, challenge or topic throughout the week?

ELEVATE

Make time to document your thoughts, and what you are observing around this topic or challenge. Remember journaling is for *you,* what you need to extract, document, apply, and grow.

☐ Check this box when you have taken and completed *one action towards this topic.*

Are you more addicted to the idea or the implementation?
Your Power Thoughts are an investment into your future self.

_____

_____

_____

_____

_____

_____

_____

_____

_____

_____

SIXTEEN

*If one advances confidently in the direction of his dreams,
and endeavors to live the life which he has imagined, he will
meet with a success unexpected in common hours.*

Henry David Thoreau

Are you CONFIDENTLY in the pursuit of a life well lived?

Such a tremendous question that unfortunately most people won't even entertain a follow-up question of why not?

Let us throw off for the moment trying to figure out ALL the details, trying to create the master blueprints, or developing the step-by-step booklet for success in our lives. Let us instead pick up the determination to simply act.

Whatever it is we dream of at night for our lives, that yearning, for a life we feel deep within us that is possible, let us awake with a fire to take steps toward our **Higher Potential**, settling for nothing less than progress.

What step will you take today?

What did you soak in from this Power Thought?

What are you going to do to engage with this thought, challenge or topic throughout the week?

ELEVATE

Make time to document your thoughts, and what you are observing around this topic or challenge. Remember journaling is for *you*, what you need to extract, document, apply, and grow.

☐ Check this box when you have taken and completed *one action towards this topic.*

Are you more addicted to the idea or the implementation?
Your Power Thoughts are an investment into your future self.

_____

_____

_____

_____

_____

_____

_____

_____

_____

_____

SEVENTEEN

If a man empties his purse into his head, no one can take it away from him. An investment in knowledge always pays the best interest.

Benjamin Franklin

Self-Assessment: How much have you invested into yourself over the last 12 months?

How does that compare to other areas of leisure or entertainment such as our cable/streaming services, unnecessary adult consumption (alcohol, having fun)?

Of course, life should have an appropriate balance, but does our life truly reflect a balance today when we compare these two?

It's no secret that the most successful people on the planet have the high commonality of investing into themselves exponentially more than the average do. Both from a time and financial standpoint. Simply put, they know they are worth the investment and thus treat their minds appropriately as their own greatest asset.

How can you begin to level up your level of intentional investment into yourself on your journey to unlocking your limitless Higher Potential?

What did you soak in from this Power Thought?

What are you going to do to engage with this thought, challenge or topic throughout the week?

ELEVATE

Make time to document your thoughts, and what you are observing around this topic or challenge. Remember journaling is for *you*, what you need to extract, document, apply, and grow.

☐ Check this box when you have taken and completed *one action towards this topic.*

Are you more addicted to the idea or the implementation?
Your Power Thoughts are an investment into your future self.

_____

_____

_____

_____

_____

_____

_____

_____

_____

EIGHTEEN

There is no passion to be found playing small – in settling for a life that is less than the one you are capable of living.

Nelson Mandela

Are you actively engaging in your fullest potential?

Not just in general as an overall aggregate of your life, but in the dissected moments of your week? On an ordinary weekday afternoon, would one find you 100% engaged and committed in the task at hand?

For most of us, we don't have to look any further than into the breakdown of our phone usage to highlight for us at minimum a starting place of opportunity to where we could redistribute time, energy, and attention into ourselves and our potential.

If we genuinely want to live the life that our higher self is calling us to, a life filled with deep and rich fulfillment and satisfaction, it will require a commitment to face head on not settling for the easy or comfortable route. Nowhere in history have we found a person who accomplished anything of admirable substance that didn't require uncomfortable sacrifice.

What is one area that you can look within and acknowledge you haven't been playing full out for and how can you engage at an elevated level as you step into your **Higher Potential**?

What did you soak in from this Power Thought?

What are you going to do to engage with this thought, challenge or topic throughout the week?

ELEVATE

Make time to document your thoughts, and what you are observing around this topic or challenge. Remember journaling is for *you*, what you need to extract, document, apply, and grow.

☐ Check this box when you have taken and completed *one action towards this topic.*

Are you more addicted to the idea or the implementation?
Your Power Thoughts are an investment into your future self.

_____

_____

_____

_____

_____

_____

_____

_____

_____

_____

NINETEEN

Most ideas are still born and need the breath of life injected into them through definite plans of immediate action. The time of nursing an idea is at the time of its birth. Every minute it lives, gives it a better chance of surviving.

Napoleon Hill

How many ideas have we never brought to fruition because we failed to breathe life into it through action?

Given that the average person has around 60,000 thoughts a day, it will never be a shortage of ideas that keeps us stagnant in life. It is the lack of will and persistence to see that idea into action.

How can you begin to capture your ideas that may be worth pursuing? What is your process, or how could you improve upon your process of seeing those ideas into action? How can you further develop your persistence of seeing these ideas all the way through?

Ideas by themselves are truly useless. Let us be inspired to cultivate this phenomenal process of creation which starts with an idea.

What did you soak in from this Power Thought?

What are you going to do to engage with this thought, challenge or topic throughout the week?

ELEVATE

Make time to document your thoughts, and what you are observing around this topic or challenge. Remember journaling is for *you*, what you need to extract, document, apply, and grow.

☐ Check this box when you have taken and completed *one action towards this topic.*

Are you more addicted to the idea or the implementation?
Your Power Thoughts are an investment into your future self.

_____

_____

_____

_____

_____

_____

_____

_____

_____

TWENTY

The number one predictor of well-being is not money or prestige, not success or accolades, but rather the time we spend with people we care about and who care about us.

Tal Ben-Shahar

In a world where we are being sold that obtaining more and working harder are the keys of a good life, it is important to truly examine the lives of those who have that as their sole focus and then reflect, is that truly the life that I want?

By no means should we aim to leave these things out of the equation necessarily, but rather making sure that our lives are designed with intention based on the life we truly desire to live.

Knowing that the #1 predictor of a life well lives is tied to the quality of our relationships, this should encourage us to make sure this is at minimum a major focus amongst the top of our priority list.

What would/could it look like to spend more quality time with those you care about the most and who also care about you? Challenge yourself to include this topic of discussion with them so that there is an elevated and mutual focus on getting even more value out of the relationship and adding intentionality to your interactions.

What did you soak in from this Power Thought?

What are you going to do to engage with this thought, challenge or topic throughout the week?

ELEVATE

Make time to document your thoughts, and what you are observing around this topic or challenge. Remember journaling is for *you*, what you need to extract, document, apply, and grow.

☐ Check this box when you have taken and completed *one action towards this topic.*

Are you more addicted to the idea or the implementation?
Your Power Thoughts are an investment into your future self.

_____

_____

_____

_____

_____

_____

_____

_____

_____

TWENTY-ONE

Go as far as you can see. When you get there, you will be able to see further.

J.P. Morgan

What is the extent of your current vision for your life?

Probably more important than this question is are you actively running towards that highest peak you can currently see?

With most of society having settled for "good enough," it is easy to see why very few people actively pursue their dreams, if they have any dreams at all.

If we would take a brief look back over our life at current, most likely we could identify things we have achieved or accomplished that at one point we'd consider to be that highest peak from a previous vantage point.

Let us look forward with even greater ambition and belief in what is possible on the horizon ahead of us.

How can you pick up the pace in going after that highest vision you currently can see? How can you reinforce the belief and knowing that even better awaits you on the other side of that peak?

What did you soak in from this Power Thought?

What are you going to do to engage with this thought, challenge or topic throughout the week?

ELEVATE

Make time to document your thoughts, and what you are observing around this topic or challenge. Remember journaling is for *you*, what you need to extract, document, apply, and grow.

☐ Check this box when you have taken and completed *one action towards this topic.*

Are you more addicted to the idea or the implementation? Your Power Thoughts are an investment into your future self.

_____

_____

_____

_____

_____

_____

_____

_____

_____

TWENTY-TWO

The mind is not a vessel to be filled but a fire to be kindled.
Bob Proctor

What fire or passion are you currently kindling in your life?

To start, those who actively engage in investing into themselves are among the minority of society. However, even smaller is the number of people who are intentionally stirring up that passion or desire in their life and thus have consciously or subconsciously accepted life simply for what it is.

The interesting thing is that we can quickly recognize in those who we'd deem as successful or living life to the fullest that a commonality is they seem to be on fire for life. This only comes by way of stirring those things up within us that in which we believe to be most important in our lives.

How can you first identify those things that are most important to you? Secondly, how can you stir those embers in that fire on a more consistent basis to keep the flame going at a level that doesn't just impact your life, but also provides that light for others?

What did you soak in from this Power Thought?

What are you going to do to engage with this thought, challenge or topic throughout the week?

ELEVATE

Make time to document your thoughts, and what you are observing around this topic or challenge. Remember journaling is for *you*, what you need to extract, document, apply, and grow.

☐ Check this box when you have taken and completed *one action towards this topic.*

Are you more addicted to the idea or the implementation?
Your Power Thoughts are an investment into your future self.

_____

_____

_____

_____

_____

_____

_____

_____

_____

_____

TWENTY-THREE

Discipline equals freedom.
Jacko Willink

What is your personal association with the word discipline?

For most of our lives, there has been such a negative relationship with discipline it is no wonder that so many people run from the word or want anything to do with it.

However, when we examine the areas of our lives where we know we aren't where we would like to be, at the root of almost all of them is because we lack self-discipline to varying degrees.

If we truly want the freedom to CHOOSE the life we desire, we must embrace and engage in discipline. Let us turn the perspective of it from something negative to the bridge necessary to get us to the life we want.

Where can you begin to engage in an elevated level of self-discipline?

What did you soak in from this Power Thought?

What are you going to do to engage with this thought, challenge or topic throughout the week?

ELEVATE

Make time to document your thoughts, and what you are observing around this topic or challenge. Remember journaling is for *you,* what you need to extract, document, apply, and grow.

☐ Check this box when you have taken and completed *one action towards this topic.*

Are you more addicted to the idea or the implementation?
Your Power Thoughts are an investment into your future self.

_____

_____

_____

_____

_____

_____

_____

_____

_____

TWENTY-FOUR

Enthusiasm is common. Endurance is rare.
Angela Duckworth

Why don't we see more doers completing the "hard things?"

A huge part is that it is just that, hard.

Everyone finds those moments in their life where they have a good idea and even many find the enthusiasm to get started. However, the statistics show the clear fact that most attempts fail.

We see this same thing every January with the mantra of a "New Year - New Me!," only to find that same habits brought into the new year equals the same you.

The real separator begins at the start from those who have an "until" mentality. Jobs not done "until" I have finished or accomplished my goal. This is critical to have upfront to be mentally prepared to endure through the known and unknown obstacles.

Once we truly have established that something is worth it, let us lock in our mindset to finish all the way "until" we get there.

How and where can you begin to turn your enthusiasm into endurance to be known as a person who keeps their word, starting with themselves, and finishes whatever they set out to accomplish?

What did you soak in from this Power Thought?

What are you going to do to engage with this thought, challenge or topic throughout the week?

ELEVATE

Make time to document your thoughts, and what you are observing around this topic or challenge. Remember journaling is for *you*, what you need to extract, document, apply, and grow.

☐ Check this box when you have taken and completed *one action towards this topic.*

**Are you more addicted to the idea or the implementation?
Your Power Thoughts are an investment into your future self.**

_____

_____

_____

_____

_____

_____

_____

_____

_____

_____

TWENTY-FIVE

*People do not decide their futures, they decide their habits
and their habits decide their futures.*

F.M. Alexander

What habits would you point to that you have intentionally designed to help you get to where you are today?

For a few of us, we could find some habits that may fit this description in helping us to arrive at this current point in life. However, almost all of us still have plenty of room for opportunity when it comes to habit building.

When unpacking the lives of the most successful people in the world, it becomes easy to see how much of their life has been designed with intention by way of the habits they build.

Given the fact that our brain LOVES habits because once a behavior is a habit it no longer has to use as much energy to get us to do the activity, shouldn't we take note and place more attention to building more habits to set us on a path toward "our" version of success?

What are a few habits you know would help the next version of you and what are a few details on how you can get started and follow-through until it is solidified part of your routine?

What did you soak in from this Power Thought?

What are you going to do to engage with this thought, challenge or topic throughout the week?

ELEVATE

Make time to document your thoughts, and what you are observing around this topic or challenge. Remember journaling is for *you*, what you need to extract, document, apply, and grow.

☐ Check this box when you have taken and completed *one action towards this topic.*

Are you more addicted to the idea or the implementation?
Your Power Thoughts are an investment into your future self.

_____

_____

_____

_____

_____

_____

_____

_____

_____

TWENTY-SIX

Do not spoil what you have by desiring what you have not;
remember that what you now have was once among the
things you only hoped for.

Epicurus

What part(s) of your life that you are currently living was once only a dream or desire?

Most of us don't do this often enough of looking back over how far we've come or how much this current version of our life is such a blessing.

Of course, we should never stop aspiring for more or creating the next level of our life that is right for us, however, let us not be so future focused that we miss sitting in true gratitude for where we are at this moment.

Having this elevated perspective will help keep us for missing the beauty and blessing of what we have in the now.

Take time to reflect on the areas of your life that you once only hoped for but is now a reality? How can you leverage this to look forward with greater confidence that the things hoped for in the future will too one day become a reality?

What did you soak in from this Power Thought?

What are you going to do to engage with this thought, challenge or topic throughout the week?

ELEVATE

Make time to document your thoughts, and what you are observing around this topic or challenge. Remember journaling is for *you*, what you need to extract, document, apply, and grow.

☐ Check this box when you have taken and completed *one action towards this topic.*

Are you more addicted to the idea or the implementation?
Your Power Thoughts are an investment into your future self.

_____

_____

_____

_____

_____

_____

_____

_____

_____

_____

TWENTY-SEVEN

Happiness is the meaning and the purpose of life, the whole aim and end of human existence.

Aristotle

What would you describe the purpose of your life to be?

Countless studies show that most people don't know what their purpose is. Part of the consequence of feeling purposeless is settling or merely accepting life "as is."

It doesn't take long to point out and/or discover how damaging this mindset is. It is at the root of why so many people have settled for just a version of what their life could be.

To be clear, this goes beyond surface level or temporary happiness. This goes into the depths of why we truly go after the things that stirs our soul. When happiness becomes the point, we'll begin to shift and shape our lives in a way that elevates the world around us because we are first elevating ourselves.

How can you first spend time identifying and discovering the things that truly makes you happy and then fold more of those action steps necessary to get there into your life?

What did you soak in from this Power Thought?

What are you going to do to engage with this thought, challenge or topic throughout the week?

ELEVATE

Make time to document your thoughts, and what you are observing around this topic or challenge. Remember journaling is for *you*, what you need to extract, document, apply, and grow.

☐ Check this box when you have taken and completed *one action towards this topic.*

Are you more addicted to the idea or the implementation?
Your Power Thoughts are an investment into your future self.

_____

_____

_____

_____

_____

_____

_____

_____

_____

TWENTY-EIGHT

To create magic in the world, focus on the magic within yourself. Look in the mirror. Your relationship with you predicts your relationship with the world. Remember that you have a primitive longing for silence and solitude, and that it is in quietude that self-awareness rises.

Robin Sharma

How much do you enjoy spending time alone with yourself?

For most of us, it can be an awkward experience spending genuine, quality time with yourself within your own mind. However, that is where true joy, happiness and success is found.

Especially in a day/age where distractions and a pulling for our attention is everywhere and ongoing, learning to get away and effectively going within is that magic that will continue to be the path of separation from living our lives by design vs. being at affect to the world around us.

How could you either start or elevate your time spent with yourself on purpose and with intention?

What did you soak in from this Power Thought?

What are you going to do to engage with this thought, challenge or topic throughout the week?

ELEVATE

Make time to document your thoughts, and what you are observing around this topic or challenge. Remember journaling is for *you,* what you need to extract, document, apply, and grow.

☐ Check this box when you have taken and completed *one action towards this topic.*

Are you more addicted to the idea or the implementation?
Your Power Thoughts are an investment into your future self.

_____

_____

_____

_____

_____

_____

_____

_____

_____

TWENTY-NINE

When you reflect on your life, ask yourself if you really chose it.

Unknown

What a PHENOMENAL question... did you CHOOSE "this" life that you are currently living?

As we are being honest with ourselves, there are most likely a few parts we have chosen but most off it has come about as a byproduct of the life set in motion from our 0-18 years of life.

This by no means is an absolving of responsibility, but rather a clear acknowledgment that if we are at or on the path to living our BEST LIFE, we should have major pause to evaluate why not and more importantly, what will it take to do so?

In a world where we do have a higher level of personal freedom, let us utilize this to the fullest and engage in the activities and mindfulness to step confidently on the path toward whatever version of living our best life may look like.

Why not?

What did you soak in from this Power Thought?

What are you going to do to engage with this thought, challenge or topic throughout the week?

ELEVATE

Make time to document your thoughts, and what you are observing around this topic or challenge. Remember journaling is for *you*, what you need to extract, document, apply, and grow.

☐ Check this box when you have taken and completed *one action towards this topic.*

Are you more addicted to the idea or the implementation? Your Power Thoughts are an investment into your future self.

_____

_____

_____

_____

_____

_____

_____

_____

_____

_____

THIRTY

What we are today comes from our thoughts of yesterday,
and our present thoughts build our life up tomorrow: our life
is the creation of our mind.

Buddha

How often are you mindfully intentional about what you are thinking about?

As you look back over our life, if we're being transparent with ourselves, we'll quickly see that our current circumstances in some way, shape, or form was brought about by the thoughts or patterns of thinking from our past.

The more important point in "this" moment is are we mostly allowing our thoughts to remain the same or are we beginning to elevate our thoughts to mimic the outcomes of the future we'd like to step into?

As we grow to become increasingly more responsible for the life we are actively creating, how can we begin to dream bigger and broader with the knowledge that our lives do indeed unfold based on what we're thinking about most of the time?

What did you soak in from this Power Thought?

What are you going to do to engage with this thought, challenge or topic throughout the week?

ELEVATE

Make time to document your thoughts, and what you are observing around this topic or challenge. Remember journaling is for *you*, what you need to extract, document, apply, and grow.

☐ Check this box when you have taken and completed *one action towards this topic.*

Are you more addicted to the idea or the implementation?
Your Power Thoughts are an investment into your future self.

_____

_____

_____

_____

_____

_____

_____

_____

_____

THIRTY-ONE

Only those who devote themselves to a cause with their whole strength and soul can be true masters. For this reason, mastery demands all of a person.

Albert Einstein

What are we giving all of ourselves to?

In a day/age where we're mostly "interested" in things and see a tremendous lack of commitment, it is easy to see why mediocrity is running rampant.

The good news is for those who find the tried-and-true way of achieving success (success defined as the progressive realization of a worthy ideal), we will find upon our path the next right step revealing itself.

What few things could you start to lock in on to gain mastery of? How could you elevate and begin to pour more of yourself into this aim?

Even if it isn't our destiny to reach the end of that mastery on those particular things, it is the process of becoming that can be universally applied and will carry us to a more fulfilled life.

What did you soak in from this Power Thought?

What are you going to do to engage with this thought, challenge or topic throughout the week?

ELEVATE

Make time to document your thoughts, and what you are observing around this topic or challenge. Remember journaling is for *you*, what you need to extract, document, apply, and grow.

☐ Check this box when you have taken and completed *one action towards this topic.*

Are you more addicted to the idea or the implementation?
Your Power Thoughts are an investment into your future self.

_____

_____

_____

_____

_____

_____

_____

_____

_____

THIRTY-TWO

*No more excuses! Do it or don't do it – but don't make excuses.
Stop using your incredible brain to think of elaborate
rationalization and justification for not taking action. Do
something. Do anything. Get on with it! Repeat to yourself;
if it's to be, it's up to me! Losers make excuses; winners
make progress.*

Brian Tracy

As Mark Twain so wisely had said, "There are 1000 excuses for failure, but never a good reason."

Our inner honesty reveals to us just how much our brain loves to come up with excuses and it's understandable why - we don't want to feel worse than necessary as to why we didn't follow through... again!

However, let us be challenged to another degree. Look back over the last few things you didn't follow through on accomplishing. What are the opportunity costs, or what have you missed out on by not accomplishing that? Who in your sphere of impact and influence didn't get to gain the benefit from you not following through?

For most of us, it is easy to let ourselves down because we've done it countless times in our lives. However, for us to forge an effective path forward of removing excuses and pushing through to get things done, we will need to leverage a deeper level of why it is important to push through when we don't feel like it. Let us grab ahold of what is said in this seed to be that winner who aims at making progress!

How can you elevate your mindset to stop making excuses and focus in on making consistent progress in the areas that will take your life to that next level?

What did you soak in from this Power Thought?

What are you going to do to engage with this thought, challenge or topic throughout the week?

ELEVATE

Make time to document your thoughts, and what you are observing around this topic or challenge. Remember journaling is for *you*, what you need to extract, document, apply, and grow.

☐ Check this box when you have taken and completed *one action towards this topic*.

Are you more addicted to the idea or the implementation?
Your Power Thoughts are an investment into your future self.

_____

_____

_____

_____

_____

_____

_____

_____

_____

_____

THIRTY-THREE

Top people are those who are more concerned with activities that are goal achieving, whereas average people are more concerned with activities that are more tension relieving.

Dennis Waitley

Success isn't a secret.

The information from an endless number of people who have succeeded in life and that we admire is available for anyone and everyone to study if they choose to.

In doing so, one would be able to come to this conclusion a major player in success is where our activities are being aimed at and for what purpose.

It is understandable with the abundance of stressors in our lives how one can fall into activities to help relieve themselves of the things they are experiencing in the moment. However, if we truly want to live a life by design and intention vs. falling victim to external circumstances, we must make the decision to alter our activities.

What are a few activities you can either begin or ones you could enhance to help drive you closer to your goals, dreams, and desires?

Let us CHOOSE to continue to reevaluate where we are spending our time and energy and in doing so become increasingly aware of how they are the primary contributor of the future we will find ourselves in.

What did you soak in from this Power Thought?

What are you going to do to engage with this thought, challenge or topic throughout the week?

ELEVATE

Make time to document your thoughts, and what you are observing around this topic or challenge. Remember journaling is for *you,* what you need to extract, document, apply, and grow.

☐ Check this box when you have taken and completed *one action towards this topic.*

Are you more addicted to the idea or the implementation?
Your Power Thoughts are an investment into your future self.

_____

_____

_____

_____

_____

_____

_____

_____

_____

THIRTY-FOUR

Remembering the why behind your actions keeps you grounded and gives you the fuel to push through difficulties.

Peter Hollins

What drives you to succeed in life?

Probably a better question is, are you truly driven to succeed in life? Given that most people do not have their own personal, custom definition of success, it becomes easy to see why so many people stop aspiring for any semblance of success and have settled into "good enough."

The reality is that anything worth having in life is going to require some level of hard work to get there. In knowing this, it sparks the question - what is it that truly drives us?

Beyond the surface level answers, we should be challenged to ask that if those things are really fuel for us, how good of a job is that fuel in pushing you to do the hard things when needed to keep moving toward?

Difficulties are a guarantee on the path toward any goal, success, or a life of true intention. Knowing and accepting this, let us not be surprised by it and instead be prepared to be victors vs. victims when they arise.

How can you go deeper and pull greater fuel from the why behind your drive? How could you increase engaging with that why daily to ensure you have enough energy for that day to do what is necessary in the moment?

Keep exploring and expanding upon this and allow those things that really matter the most in life to you be the thing you can grab onto when you need because we all need it!

What did you soak in from this Power Thought?

What are you going to do to engage with this thought, challenge or topic throughout the week?

ELEVATE

Make time to document your thoughts, and what you are observing around this topic or challenge. Remember journaling is for *you,* what you need to extract, document, apply, and grow.

☐ Check this box when you have taken and completed *one action towards this topic.*

Are you more addicted to the idea or the implementation?
Your Power Thoughts are an investment into your future self.

_____

_____

_____

_____

_____

_____

_____

_____

_____

_____

THIRTY-FIVE

The only person you are destined to become is the person you decide to be.

Ralph Waldo Emerson

Who have you decided to be in life?

The better or precursor question for most probably should be - have you decided who you want to be in life?

If we can step outside of ourselves in the moment and examine the timeline of our life, it becomes easy to realize just how much of our life happened by way of simply being in certain environments and being around other people.

By our very nature, we are mimicking machines. We adapt to the people and environments we find ourselves in, mostly unknowingly. We think and believe we have the power of choice but viewing our life from this timeline perspective, we can quickly see how much of those choices where a byproduct of our environments.

As you continue to navigate your life forward, how can you begin to step outside of your habitual way of thinking and doing things to make sure you are truly directing your thoughts and actions toward the life you want?

As you do this, ensure you are spending time to think through and dream of the life you want and the person in that vision who you would have to be to live that type of life. This is becoming the master of your destiny.

What did you soak in from this Power Thought?

What are you going to do to engage with this thought, challenge or topic throughout the week?

ELEVATE

Make time to document your thoughts, and what you are observing around this topic or challenge. Remember journaling is for *you*, what you need to extract, document, apply, and grow.

☐ Check this box when you have taken and completed *one action towards this topic.*

Are you more addicted to the idea or the implementation?
Your Power Thoughts are an investment into your future self.

_____

_____

_____

_____

_____

_____

_____

_____

_____

_____

THIRTY-SIX

The great tragedy of life is not death but what we allowed to die inside of us while we live.

Norman Cousins

Are you truly living?

If someone followed you around for an entire week, how would they describe our life based on the things they have witnessed?

Whether it is your overall happiness, positive and good energy, or level of engagement, what parts of how we go about living on a daily/weekly basis is intentionally being lived out in the moment with purpose?

It doesn't take long to recognize that justifying and living "good enough" is happening all around us. However, for those of us who know deep within that better is possible, let us CHOOSE to carve out a different life. One designed on purpose.

How can you begin to examine your life at a deeper level to identify where to begin living more in the moment with passion and zeal?

Whatever it is, make the commitment to begin elevating your expectations and follow-through to live a life worth living!

What did you soak in from this Power Thought?

What are you going to do to engage with this thought, challenge or topic throughout the week?

ELEVATE

Make time to document your thoughts, and what you are observing around this topic or challenge. Remember journaling is for *you*, what you need to extract, document, apply, and grow.

☐ Check this box when you have taken and completed *one action towards this topic.*

Are you more addicted to the idea or the implementation? Your Power Thoughts are an investment into your future self.

_____

_____

_____

_____

_____

_____

_____

_____

_____

THIRTY-SEVEN

The reasonable man adapts himself to the world; the unreasonable one persists in trying to adapt the world to himself. Therefore, all progress depends on the unreasonable man.

George Bernard Shaw

How much of your life have you designed vs. simply adapted to the world?

No one likes to admit that we've allowed ourselves to be so influenced by the world that we are not in control of our life. Yet, look around and really ask is this the version people would have chosen?

It is easy to understand how this happens as there is a social reward for falling in line with the average among us. You're not at the bottom yet won't be ridiculed or have to do the hard work necessary to separate yourself into the upper part of society.

The real question is however... what do YOU truly want for your life?

Odds are, if any of us spend real alone time getting intimate with our higher selves, we will feel that calling for the next level of our life because our inner being desires to expand into becoming all you are capable of being.

How can you either begin or elevate how you are going about adopting the world to the life you want to design for you vs. the other way around?

In going down this journey, you will continue to feel an aliveness that will encourage you to keep going as there is never a "there" or destination, rather a knowing that I Am on the path. And that will become enough...

What did you soak in from this Power Thought?

What are you going to do to engage with this thought, challenge or topic throughout the week?

ELEVATE

Make time to document your thoughts, and what you are observing around this topic or challenge. Remember journaling is for *you,* what you need to extract, document, apply, and grow.

☐ Check this box when you have taken and completed *one action towards this topic.*

Are you more addicted to the idea or the implementation? Your Power Thoughts are an investment into your future self.

_____

_____

_____

_____

_____

_____

_____

_____

_____

_____

THIRTY-EIGHT

We could never learn to be brave and patient if there were only joy in the world.

Helen Keller

Through life's ups and downs, how have you been evolving your perspective?

When we really boil down the core differences in everyone's "reality," perspective is one of the base ingredients that feeds and fuels into the level of our experience.

Of course, no one loves going through adversities in life, however those are most often the best teachers. We don't love being sick but only appreciate health to the degree we do in contrast to not being healthy.

The list could go on and on which only drives the point, life is so much more about how we CHOOSE to go through what is happening to us than the actual event itself.

Knowing this, how can you begin to lean into these moments more often with the mindset of growing from adversity rather than focusing on the negative in certain circumstances?

What did you soak in from this Power Thought?

What are you going to do to engage with this thought, challenge or topic throughout the week?

ELEVATE

Make time to document your thoughts, and what you are observing around this topic or challenge. Remember journaling is for *you*, what you need to extract, document, apply, and grow.

☐ Check this box when you have taken and completed *one action towards this topic.*

Are you more addicted to the idea or the implementation?
Your Power Thoughts are an investment into your future self.

_____

_____

_____

_____

_____

_____

_____

_____

_____

_____

THIRTY-NINE

The making of a masterpiece is much less about the cash to be made and much more about the character of the creator.

Robin Sharma

Are you more focused on character building or career development currently in your life?

This quote is often only fully understood by those who have experienced more of life. The question is, if so many people that have lived this experience out are all saying the same thing to the next generation, why aren't more people paying attention?

We know that social media has a major part in fueling people's dissatisfaction, therefore how do we begin to separate what it is we truly want which will then follow what character traits we should be working on and strengthening.

If making a masterpiece of our life was possible, and why wouldn't it be, how can we begin to redirect more of our energy, effort and focus on character building first?

The after affects will come along the way in its right timing as we prepare ourselves to live out that life in advance when we stop focusing as much on what we're getting and more on who we are becoming.

What did you soak in from this Power Thought?

What are you going to do to engage with this thought, challenge or topic throughout the week?

ELEVATE

Make time to document your thoughts, and what you are observing around this topic or challenge. Remember journaling is for *you*, what you need to extract, document, apply, and grow.

☐ Check this box when you have taken and completed *one action towards this topic.*

Are you more addicted to the idea or the implementation?
Your Power Thoughts are an investment into your future self.

_____

_____

_____

_____

_____

_____

_____

_____

_____

_____

FORTY

I have had dreams and I've had nightmares. I have conquered my nightmares because of my dreams.

Jonas Salk

Which of these two, dreams or nightmares (fears) are more active in your life?

We know that fear is probably the number one obstacle for most people to overcome in trying to reach their dreams. It is often so powerful that most of society doesn't even dream anymore.

However, regardless of where we have fallen on that spectrum, let us be challenged to study the lives the doers and successful people we know.

What we are sure to find is that it isn't some special talent or unique thing about them that got them there, it was their willingness to give themselves permission to dream and more importantly, they simply committed to taking action until their dreams came true.

How can you either start dreaming again or expand your current dreams even further? What fear stands in the way of us truly following-through to bring it to a reality?

What did you soak in from this Power Thought?

What are you going to do to engage with this thought, challenge or topic throughout the week?

ELEVATE

Make time to document your thoughts, and what you are observing around this topic or challenge. Remember journaling is for *you*, what you need to extract, document, apply, and grow.

◻ Check this box when you have taken and completed *one action towards this topic.*

Are you more addicted to the idea or the implementation?
Your Power Thoughts are an investment into your future self.

_____

_____

_____

_____

_____

_____

_____

_____

_____

FORTY-ONE

Treat people as if they were what they ought to be, and you help them become what they are capable of becoming.

Johann von Goethe

When was the last time you truly evaluated how you engage with others, especially those closest to you?

If we can step back and see the reality of how much of society is hindered by a lack of self-confidence, it becomes easy to see just how powerful and needed it is to help raise up people's confidence and self-esteem.

Even if we ourselves find that we may be lacking in this area at times, one of the best ways to elevate our lives is to intentionally lift those around us.

This serves two primary purposes. First, it feels good to help others and therefore we are engaging in feel-good activities. Second, rising tides lift all boats so the better we help others become, that in turn will reciprocate back into our lives.

How can we begin to look within our sphere of influence in our lives and identify a few people that we will commit to pouring into and helping them see their higher potential and who they are capable of becoming? What does that look like, sound like, and feel like?

Let us not fall in life with the status quo of simply allowing people around us to struggle through life when we have the gift and ability to help raise expectations, beliefs and confidence that better is possible.

What did you soak in from this Power Thought?

What are you going to do to engage with this thought, challenge or topic throughout the week?

ELEVATE

Make time to document your thoughts, and what you are observing around this topic or challenge. Remember journaling is for *you*, what you need to extract, document, apply, and grow.

☐ Check this box when you have taken and completed *one action towards this topic.*

Are you more addicted to the idea or the implementation?
Your Power Thoughts are an investment into your future self.

_____

_____

_____

_____

_____

_____

_____

_____

_____

_____

FORTY-TWO

A clear plan relieves you of the torment of choice.
Saul Bellow

Do you have a CLEAR plan for your life?

This is an interesting and challenging question. Even for the few that would say yes, just how clear is it and are you actively following it daily?

For most, we would recognize an opportunity to either develop a plan or at minimum spend time tweaking the one we have currently.

Simply realizing that most people truly fail to plan thus plan to fail, shouldn't this be the indicator that if we too don't want to fall in line among the average who merely wish for things in life vs. the ones who obtain them that we must develop ourselves into these higher levels of engaging in life?

What does a level up plan for your life look like right now? Take some time to develop at least seeds for it to start with? How can you engage with it more often to ensure actual follow-through?

As we navigate our lives daily, have the honesty required to make sure we avoid falling into the trap of "good enough." Set regular reminders for your commitment to executing on your plan for a great life.

What did you soak in from this Power Thought?

What are you going to do to engage with this thought, challenge or topic throughout the week?

ELEVATE

Make time to document your thoughts, and what you are observing around this topic or challenge. Remember journaling is for *you*, what you need to extract, document, apply, and grow.

☐ Check this box when you have taken and completed *one action towards this topic.*

Are you more addicted to the idea or the implementation?
Your Power Thoughts are an investment into your future self.

_____

_____

_____

_____

_____

_____

_____

_____

_____

_____

FORTY-THREE

Don't ever diminish the power of words. Words move hearts and hearts move limbs.

Hamza Yusuf

What amount of life are you speaking into others and more importantly into yourself on a regular basis?

Over our lifetime we have seen the power of words from both a positive and negative standpoint. Yet despite knowing this, have you ever considered why we don't leverage this power that is available to every single person more often?

Though there are a lot of contributing factors to this, one of the primary reasons is as mimicking machines we mostly adapt into the environments that already exist. Thus, if it isn't common practice amongst us, then few step forward with the effort to utilize it in their lives.

The underlying question then becomes, do we want to live a life on par with what common among us? Odds are if you're reading this book, you desire more for your life.

How can you begin to speak more positively and proactively into the lives of those around you more often? How can you level up your own inner dialogue to speak life into yourself multiple times a day more than you are now?

By engaging in this simple practice with intention, we will begin to raise up those around us and in reciprocal fashion improve our own trajectory to a life well lived.

What did you soak in from this Power Thought?

What are you going to do to engage with this thought, challenge or topic throughout the week?

ELEVATE

Make time to document your thoughts, and what you are observing around this topic or challenge. Remember journaling is for *you*, what you need to extract, document, apply, and grow.

☐ Check this box when you have taken and completed *one action towards this topic.*

Are you more addicted to the idea or the implementation?
Your Power Thoughts are an investment into your future self.

_____

_____

_____

_____

_____

_____

_____

_____

_____

FORTY-FOUR

Any successful person has to decide what to do in part by deciding what not to do.

Angela Duckworth

How often are you evaluating and more importantly eliminating activities that aren't fruitful in your life?

Along our journey of growth, develop, and success, it is easy to get wrapped up in things that are good in the moment but may not serve as the best use of your time in the long run.

Initially being asked to be involved in so many things feel good and is flattering, but if we genuinely want to be our best and live our best lives, we must learn the art and skill of choosing the "right" activities that are "right" for us.

With an endless amount of things we could spend our time on, giving this area appropriate focus is crucial. Though time is free, it is our most precious resource. How we choose to spend our free time will determine how valuable we become.

How can you begin or elevate your evaluation of where and how you are spending your time? Do these activities align with your overall ideals and values? How can you begin to redistribute your time into more fruitful activities?

In examining the lives of those who are seemingly living their best life, being the master of their time is one of the most common traits we will find. Let us too commit to following suite.

What did you soak in from this Power Thought?

What are you going to do to engage with this thought, challenge or topic throughout the week?

ELEVATE

Make time to document your thoughts, and what you are observing around this topic or challenge. Remember journaling is for *you*, what you need to extract, document, apply, and grow.

☐ Check this box when you have taken and completed *one action towards this topic.*

Are you more addicted to the idea or the implementation?
Your Power Thoughts are an investment into your future self.

_____

_____

_____

_____

_____

_____

_____

_____

_____

_____

FORTY-FIVE

Courage is rightly considered the foremost of the virtues, for upon it, all others depend.

Winston Churchill

How courageously are you engaging with life?

The reality of being human is that we all experience fear because it is deeply wired into our biology.

The impacting question is, are we allowing it to hold us back or are we pushing through to get to the other side of the things and the life we really want?

Unfortunately for most, they become so crippled by fear that they simply fail to act, which becomes the root of settling in so many areas of life.

How can you begin to step more courageously into those moments and areas of your life that we know deep within us have been holding us back?

Once you've identified a few areas, look for an accountability partner to share with because we need others outside of us to make sure we begin to level up our accountability. If you don't do this simple thing, there goes your cowardice showing up again!

What did you soak in from this Power Thought?

What are you going to do to engage with this thought, challenge or topic throughout the week?

ELEVATE

Make time to document your thoughts, and what you are observing around this topic or challenge. Remember journaling is for *you,* what you need to extract, document, apply, and grow.

☐ Check this box when you have taken and completed *one action towards this topic.*

Are you more addicted to the idea or the implementation?
Your Power Thoughts are an investment into your future self.

_____

_____

_____

_____

_____

_____

_____

_____

_____

FORTY-SIX

Persistence is to the character of man as carbon is to steal.

Napoleon Hill

On a scale of 1-10, where would you rate your level of persistence or tenacity today?

Practically every one of us could identify where we could use a little (or a lot) more persistence. Looking back, we all can recognize how many times in our lives we've quit too early on something only to think in the now and realize "what if I would have stayed with that!"

Reflection isn't meant to stir up regret but rather fuel an alternate or elevated path forward.

What would improving upon your current level of persistence look like? Knowing some of the challenging obstacles in your path, how can you begin to plan ahead of time as to how you will CHOOSE to persist through them?

We know there is no easy path to reaching success, thus let us embrace the need to develop persistence and actively engage in it become our push through factor.

What did you soak in from this Power Thought?

What are you going to do to engage with this thought, challenge or topic throughout the week?

ELEVATE

Make time to document your thoughts, and what you are observing around this topic or challenge. Remember journaling is for *you*, what you need to extract, document, apply, and grow.

☐ Check this box when you have taken and completed *one action towards this topic.*

Are you more addicted to the idea or the implementation?
Your Power Thoughts are an investment into your future self.

_____

_____

_____

_____

_____

_____

_____

_____

_____

FORTY-SEVEN

The most precious gift we can offer others is our presence.
When mindfulness embraces those we love, they will bloom
like flowers.

Thich Nhat Hanh

In our world of endless distractions, how present are you truly in the moments with those that matter the most to you in your life?

This should be a question we challenge ourselves with and reflect upon on a regular basis for we all know how easy it is to get swept up into the distraction vortex of life.

We see this more and more evident in the world around us going out to eat, in meetings, and even spending that precious alone time with those you love the most.

Shouldn't we begin to elevate our expectations if we truly want to foster deeper and more quality connection with those we say we care about the most in life?

How can you first become more aware and honest about where you have opportunities to improve in this space? Second, how can you begin to improve upon what you have taken notice of to become known as a person who is fully present when in the presence of others?

Now more than ever, this beautiful gift is needed in our world. Let us make the commitment to be this type of blessing to those we engage with daily.

What did you soak in from this Power Thought?

What are you going to do to engage with this thought, challenge or topic throughout the week?

ELEVATE

Make time to document your thoughts, and what you are observing around this topic or challenge. Remember journaling is for *you,* what you need to extract, document, apply, and grow.

☐ Check this box when you have taken and completed *one action towards this topic.*

Are you more addicted to the idea or the implementation?
Your Power Thoughts are an investment into your future self.

_____

_____

_____

_____

_____

_____

_____

_____

_____

FORTY-EIGHT

Commit to seeing pain in a new way, as a super important message delivery system. Listen to the pain and learn what it is telling you.

Trent Shelton

What lessons has pain taught you over your life?

Though we know that there is no avoiding pain completely in life, it is unfortunate how often we don't reflect to gain valuable insight to how we can learn and grow from the pain we experience.

Many even become so crippled by their pain that they become hindered to various degrees that prevents them from stepping into their next level of greatness in their lives.

Let us DECIDE to stop fighting the great teacher that pain can be and instead trade our why's for what's. Let us stop asking dis-empowering questions like "Why is this happening to me?" and instead ask "What can I learn from this?"

How can you first, spend some time reflecting over some of the pain you have experienced in life and ask yourself if there are things missing that could be learned from it? Second, how can you improve upon your reflection in the moment of experiencing pain to not only help get you through it faster, but also ensure there is a lesson learned in each new moment?

The more we can cultivate this type of mindset, the better it will help to automatically help feed and fuel our overall growth in life.

What did you soak in from this Power Thought?

What are you going to do to engage with this thought, challenge or topic throughout the week?

ELEVATE

Make time to document your thoughts, and what you are observing around this topic or challenge. Remember journaling is for *you*, what you need to extract, document, apply, and grow.

☐ Check this box when you have taken and completed
one action towards this topic.

Are you more addicted to the idea or the implementation?
Your Power Thoughts are an investment into your future self.

_____

_____

_____

_____

_____

_____

_____

_____

_____

_____

FORTY-NINE

Can you learn to witness your life rather than identify with it? Believe it or not, that's where bliss resides, where higher awareness resides, where authentic freedom resides.

Brendon Burchard

How often are you objectively stepping outside of your daily grind to zoom out and view your life from a broader vantage point?

For most of us, the answer would be probably not enough. With an endless amount of things we "could" do, it is very easy to get swept up in the daily undertow of life happening.

Looking around and recognizing this very thing in most of the people you engage with on a regular basis, how well is this strategy working out for others in their lives?"

Learning to observe this more often and at a deeper level should help us to better reflect inward to our own lives and ask that similar question, is this the life I truly want to be living?

How can you first become more aware of how you are engaging with your life at current? Next, in more of the moments within your days/ weeks, how can you create more moments to simply pause and step into higher awareness to help ensure that you have the appropriate perspective and that you are indeed headed in the direction you are desiring to go in life?

As we do this, not only will we level up our life, but we will also become beacons for others to witness the limitless potential of living a life by design.

What did you soak in from this Power Thought?

What are you going to do to engage with this thought, challenge or topic throughout the week?

ELEVATE

Make time to document your thoughts, and what you are observing around this topic or challenge. Remember journaling is for *you*, what you need to extract, document, apply, and grow.

☐ Check this box when you have taken and completed *one action towards this topic.*

Are you more addicted to the idea or the implementation?
Your Power Thoughts are an investment into your future self.

_____

_____

_____

_____

_____

_____

_____

_____

_____

_____

FIFTY

Independent of others and in concert with others, your main task in life is to do what you can best do and become what you can potentially be.

Erich Fromm

Are you "actively" pursuing being the absolute best version of yourself that you can become?

If no, why not? If yes, what evidence would you have to support that indeed you are in the constant pursuit of reaching your fullest potential?

I would gauge to say that anyone reading this book, probably falls somewhere in between, closer to the spectrum of pursuing their best life. (Who else reads books on elevating their life?)

One point of observation is just how much of society falls in line with what the majority of society is doing. It is clear in almost every part of life. Therefore, we must accept that the journey to become our best selves is often one traveled by only a few.

If we indeed have the stomach for that, let us challenge ourselves in every area of our life, what would the "next best version" of me look like in this area. Reflect on a few key areas of your life asking that question and begin writing details out about what it looks like and more importantly how you could begin to take steps toward becoming that.

For those who can get a glimpse of what life would look like on the other side of this worthy pursuit, that vision becomes fuel needed to step into our next version of what we are capable of becoming.

What did you soak in from this Power Thought?

What are you going to do to engage with this thought, challenge or topic throughout the week?

ELEVATE

Make time to document your thoughts, and what you are observing around this topic or challenge. Remember journaling is for *you*, what you need to extract, document, apply, and grow.

☐ Check this box when you have taken and completed
one action towards this topic.

Are you more addicted to the idea or the implementation?
Your Power Thoughts are an investment into your future self.

_____

_____

_____

_____

_____

_____

_____

_____

_____

_____

FIFTY-ONE

One who sweats more in training bleeds less in war.
Spartan Warrior credo

What does your current training regimen look like to help you win at life?

Too often we only think of training as something physical, when real training for a successful life has far more to do with how we are training ourselves mentally.

We know that we have a much more reactive society than a proactive one. Thus, we can see why most are allowing life to happen to them vs. truly going after what they want.

The basis to a great life starts with spending time defining what you want. Behind this is getting brutally honest about what it will take to reach that type of life. From here challenging yourself of - are you willing to put the real work in that necessary to get there?

If yes, get moving. If no, readjust your expectations and desires in life.

How can you begin to improve upon training yourself in various parts of your life so that you are battle ready to conquer the tough moments that will come to test your will and resolve to see if you truly want to reach that next level?

Knowing how much we admire those who have accomplished great things by pushing through life's adversities, let us CHOOSE to become one ourselves with this first step of training ourselves.

What did you soak in from this Power Thought?

What are you going to do to engage with this thought, challenge or topic throughout the week?

ELEVATE

Make time to document your thoughts, and what you are observing around this topic or challenge. Remember journaling is for *you,* what you need to extract, document, apply, and grow.

☐ Check this box when you have taken and completed *one action towards this topic.*

Are you more addicted to the idea or the implementation? Your Power Thoughts are an investment into your future self.

_____

_____

_____

_____

_____

_____

_____

_____

_____

_____

FIFTY-TWO

To live in the hearts we leave behind is not to die.

Thomas Campbell

How do you think about your legacy? (If at all)

When we step back from all our daily activities, the things we say yes to, and everything that we allow to fill our calendars, what is it all for?

Far too often, people simply step out into life, get a job, start a family, and once they get pulled into the matrix, they potentially aspire to level up here and there, but mostly accept life as it is.

But again, why and for what?

The best part about thinking on our legacy is that we still have time to decide what we'd like it to be and thus have time to create action steps to influence what our legacy will become.

Ultimately, our legacy won't simply be defined by us, but by the impact, stories, and views others had about us. However, we can ensure that we spend intentional time writing quality moments upon the hearts and minds that we most care about and interact with daily.

How can you elevate how you currently think about your legacy? From there, how can you begin to ensure this thoughtful mindfulness is a part of how you are designing your life going forward?

Let this be a major part of our "for what" and a huge part of the outcome will be an increased daily life worth every minute of living it.

What did you soak in from this Power Thought?

What are you going to do to engage with this thought, challenge or topic throughout the week?

ELEVATE

Make time to document your thoughts, and what you are observing around this topic or challenge. Remember journaling is for *you*, what you need to extract, document, apply, and grow.

☐ Check this box when you have taken and completed *one action towards this topic.*

Are you more addicted to the idea or the implementation?
Your Power Thoughts are an investment into your future self.

_____

_____

_____

_____

_____

_____

_____

_____

_____

WINS

MILE MARKERS –
THE MOMENTUM
OF SUCCESS

Let's face it, most of us are bad at noticing and celebrating our wins.

In fact, most of society is bad at this, choosing more often to pay attention to crisis and failure. Listen, if you aren't intentionally noticing when and how often you're winning, you're missing out!

It's easier to build momentum when you can see how often you're moving forward. It's like looking up after working on something for a long time to see just how far you've come. The truth is WINS are like oxygen - they fuel our dreams.

Take time to notice, name, and celebrate your wins. Write down what it was, how it benefits you, and how you feel after it!

PERSONAL   PROFESSIONAL   POTENTIAL

letsthink3d.com